MASTER YOUR LIFE

PSYCHOLOGICALLY
GROW IN LIFE WITH THE
WISDOM OF 100% SCIENTIFIC THEORIES

ROZZE S. BALENG

Thank you, in alphabetical order:

Arsalan Labaf and Siavash Habibi	for inspirational trialogue.
Hélène Ahlström Fryxell	for autonomy.
Loulou & Lorentz	for patience.
Mamiljou	for life.
Nastaran Baleng-Soultani	for consideration and support.
Jose Pepito and Jonas Lagergren	for design and creativity

ABOUT THE AUTHOR

Rozze S. Baleng is the consultant that went from practicing law and business, to later switch to human development and organization, and from there subsequently landed in that "agile coaching" that is where he can contribute to growth the most. As such he has successfully helped aspirational leaders and teams in different organizations to both improve growth and value, and to find bottlenecks and hinders in their processes. Very often in a scientific approach where a solution to a problem is merely a hypothesis that has to be tried out before trying another successful approach forward. All his practical and spiritual work is more or less founded on the scientific theories found in this book.

Rozze has University degrees in both Psychology (B.Sc) and Law (LL.M), and is a Certified Agile Coach (ICF-ACC, PSM I, ICP-ACC/ATF).

You may contact Rozze by email rozze@baleng.se or visit his profile on Linkedin: http://linkedin.com/in/rozzebaleng

FOREWORD

I write this foreword sitting in my kitchen in the mountain resort of Åre, Sweden. The landscape around me is a breathtaking canvas of winter's touch. As part of my shamanic life path, I've been called up here to connect more deeply with myself, humanity and nature. It's January, and the world here is enveloped in a pristine blanket of snow, transforming the rugged terrain into a serene wonderland. The sky above is a brilliant blue and clear, with clouds painting fleeting shadows on the snow-clad mountains. This setting is a perfect backdrop for contemplating the depths of human experience. However, it is perhaps not the most logical backdrop for thinking about elephants. Yet, I find myself sitting here thinking about just that. Elephants.

More specifically, I find myself contemplating the famous Buddhist story of the Blind Men and the Elephant. In this story, a group of blind men touch different parts of an elephant to learn what it is like. Each man feels a different part, such as the trunk or the tusk, and concludes that the elephant is like a rope or a spear, respectively. This story illustrates the idea that truth can be perceived in different ways depending on one's perspective and experience. It teaches the importance of recognizing that there are many ways to understand the world and underscores the value of exploring one's own path to understanding. I find this story to be a relevant analogy to guide us into this book that you're about to read. "Master Your Life Psychologically" invites you to explore many different approaches to understanding a very specific version of the elephant story – the version where the elephant is you.

In our world brimming with complexity and constant change, "Master Your Life Psychologically," with its compendium of 100 psychological theories, provides a unique lens for understanding the human mind and behavior. This makes it an indispensable tool for therapists, coaches, educators, and anyone interested in personal growth. The book invites us to explore the intricate workings of the mind, offering valuable insights for navigating life's challenges.

As a corporate shamanic practitioner, my role is to bridge the realms of business and innovation with spirituality and introspection. My commitment to doing this bridging work is also why I like this book. This is a book of bridges leading not only into oneself, but hopefully also into a deeper understanding of our interconnectedness with all living things and all aspects of life. The way we show up at home, at work, and in our relationships reflects and influences the larger world. By exploring ourselves, we find paths towards a future where living in harmony with nature and each other is not just a dream but a sustainable reality.

What I also enjoy is that the book's structure allows for both a systematic approach and a playful exploration of self. Setting an intention or a question and randomly picking a page or theory can lead to unexpected insights and spiritual growth. It can serve as both a guide and a companion in your journey, providing scientific grounding and spiritual enrichment. And to add an intriguing twist to the story, Rozze invited me to contribute a theory to the book, Meadow Mapping (please enjoy!) - one that, admittedly, lacks the scientific rigor of the others. To me, this inclusion serves a pivotal purpose: to underscore the notion that while science is a vital tool in our quest for understanding, the exploration of the human psyche transcends empirical evidence. It's a realm where intuition, experience, and the myriad facets of human consciousness converge, reminding us that the journey to self-understanding is infinite, evolving with humanity itself. We will never be able to experience the whole elephant, yet our continued work of exploring it is perhaps the most important work there is.

So with that, I urge you to go explore your own inner elephant throughout the pages of this book.

With love
/Nils von Heijne, human being and explorer of corporate shamanism
nilsvonheijne.com

INTRODUCTION

Welcome to "Master Your Life - Psychologically: Grow in life through 100+ scientific theories," an all-encompassing guidebook designed to help you transform your life and achieve personal growth. In today's fast-paced world, it can be challenging to navigate life's obstacles and attain your goals. You may often feel overwhelmed, lost, or stuck in a rut. However, there is good news: scientific theories exist that can assist you in overcoming these obstacles and living a more fulfilling life.

This book explores over 100 scientifically-backed theories that can help you overcome hurdles and improve your life. By delving into the fascinating world of psychology, this book provides practical tools and techniques for you to master your life.

Throughout the following chapters, you will be encouraged to take an active role in your personal growth. This book emphasizes the importance of self-reflection and self-awareness, underlining the value of taking responsibility for your own life. This empowering approach encourages you to take control of your life and achieve your goals.

The chapters explore a variety of theories and concepts, including cognitive-behavioral therapy, positive psychology, emotional intelligence, and many others. The clear and concise structure of the book makes it easy to navigate and understand, ensuring that you can easily integrate these theories into your life.

With "Master Your Life - Psychologically: Grow in life through 100+ scientific theories," you can unlock your full potential and achieve your dreams. This book is a must-read for anyone looking to live a more fulfilling and satisfying life.

CONTENTS

COGNITIVE AND PERCEPTUAL BIASES

ACTOR-OBSERVER BIAS

The Actor-Observer Bias is when we explain our own actions based on external factors, like the situation we're in, but we explain other people's actions based on their personality or character. This was studied by Lee Ross, who had people rate the reasons for a conversation between two people. People who played one of the people in the conversation said their behavior was because of what was happening around them, but they said the other person's behavior was because of who they are.

For example, if you trip and fall, you might blame it on the ground being slippery, but if someone else trips and falls, you might think they are clumsy.

QUESTIONS

1. How might the actor-observer bias affect your interpretation of your own actions compared to those of others in your personal relationships or professional life?

2. Can you identify a situation in which you attributed your behaviour to external factors while judging another's behaviour to be due to their personality or character? How can recognising this bias improve your understanding of the situation?

3. How can you show empathy and understanding for others by taking into account the biases of actors and observers in your daily life?

ANCHORING BIAS THEORY

Daniel Kahneman and Amos Tversky first published Anchoring Bias Theory in 1974. It is a cognitive behavioral theory that states people tend to focus on a particular aspect of information when making decisions and establishing a numerical assessment, regardless of its relevance to the problem. This is known as an anchor, which establishes a context for decision-making and interpreting other related information.

An example of anchoring bias in real life is when someone is shopping for goods or services they are unfamiliar with. They use the first price they see as an anchor and interpret the following prices based on that point of reference. The individual might find a much better option at a reduced price but will feel uneasy about spending more than the initial anchor they established.

QUESTIONS

1. Can you recall a situation where you relied too much on an initial piece of information (the "anchor") when making a decision? How might this have affected the outcome?

2. How can you develop a more balanced approach to decision-making by considering multiple perspectives and sources of information?

3. What strategies can you use to minimise the influence of anchoring bias in your personal and professional life?

ATTRIBUTION BIAS THEORY

Attribution Bias Theory is a theory published in 1973 by psychologist Fritz Heider. This theory explains how people tend to make attributions or judgments to explain events in their environment. According to the theory, people observe a situation, draw conclusions based on their mental models, then attribute a cause to the behavior they observe. In the world of attribution bias, people tend to focus on one factor and draw conclusions about the cause that fit their preconceived assumptions or beliefs.

For example, suppose a salesman failed to make a sale. In that case, the manager can attribute that failure to the salesman's lack of communication skills when multiple factors, such as market conditions, customer preferences, product price, etc., may have also been involved in the decision-making process. In addition, individuals are often biased to blame external factors for failures or successes instead of internal ones, such as their attitude or lack of motivation.

QUESTIONS

1. Can you name a recent situation in which you may have made an incorrect assumption about another person's behavior or motives? What factors might have contributed to this attribution error?

2. How can being aware of your biased perception help you to develop more empathy and understanding for others?

3. What steps can you take to challenge your initial assumptions and consider alternative explanations for others' actions?

AVAILABILITY BIAS

Availability bias is a cognitive bias where people are more likely to make decisions based on the most readily available information. Scientists Amos Tversky and Daniel Kahneman established this theory in the 1970s.

People process information more readily and remember events that stand out instead of accurately evaluating the situation. This can create a distorted view of reality, as other important information is overlooked.

When someone decides how to invest their money, they may recall a personal story they heard of someone who invested in stocks and made a large return. However, the individual may overlook the other examples of people investing in the same stocks with less successful results.

If someone is asked to estimate the likelihood of a particular event, they may rely on examples that come to mind easily, such as recent news stories or personal experiences, rather than taking into account all relevant statistics or information.

Availability bias can lead to inaccurate judgments and decisions, as important information may be overlooked or weighted incorrectly. It is important to be aware of this bias and to seek out diverse sources of information when making decisions or forming opinions.

QUESTIONS

1. How might availability bias affect your perception of risks, opportunities or the likelihood of certain events in your life?

2. Can you recall a situation where availability bias might have led you to make a wrong judgment or decision? How might a more comprehensive view have changed your approach?

3. What strategies can you use to ensure that you consider a wide range of information and experiences rather than just relying on what comes readily to mind?

AVAILABILITY CASCADE

The Availability Cascade is a theory proposed by Timur Kuran in 1995. It explains how false ideas often become accepted as true in society. The theory suggests that information presented in the media or announced frequently by influential people (and assumed to be true) will become more available due to its frequency. This often results in more people believing the idea because it has become so easily accessible.

An example of the availability cascade in action is the release of the movie The Social Network, which portrays Mark Zuckerberg as a villain who stole the idea of Facebook from his Harvard classmates. This portrayal of Zuckerberg in popular media caused many individuals to believe he had acted dishonestly despite evidence to the contrary.

QUESTIONS

1. How have you observed the availability cascade in your life, for example, in forming your opinions or beliefs about certain topics?

2. Can you name an instance in which you have unknowingly contributed to the propagation of an availability cascade? How might this awareness affect your approach to sharing information?

3. How can you develop critical thinking skills to recognize and challenge the validity of availability cascades in your personal and professional life?

AVAILABILITY HEURISTIC

The availability heuristic was coined by psychologists Amos Tversky and Daniel Kahneman in the 1970s.

The availability heuristic is a mental shortcut that relies on immediate examples that come to mind when evaluating a particular decision or situation. When an individual accesses a mental shortcut, they are more likely to make decisions quickly but with a higher chance of errors in judgment.

An example would be when an individual may feel that something is more likely to happen if they can more easily recall similar events. For example, with news stories of shark attacks, an individual may become fearful of swimming in the ocean if they can easily recall stories of these attacks, even if they know the chances of it happening are close to zero.

QUESTIONS

1. To what extent have you experienced availability heuristics influencing your decisions or judgments?

2. How can you broaden your perspective and consider a wider range of information when making decisions or forming opinions rather than relying on the most readily available information?

3. What techniques can you use to counteract the avail-ability heuristic and make better-informed decisions in your life?

BIAS BLIND SPOT THEORY

P. E. Tetlock and MaiTai Li first proposed Bias Blind Spot Theory in 1995. It suggests that while people recognize the potential biases of others, they usually do not recognize their own biases. This is based on an illusion of objectivity, wherein people tend to over-rely on their perspectives leading them to overlook their biases.

The theory further states that the higher an individual's self-esteem, the lower their ability to accurately identify the potential biases in their judgment. The authors of the theory term this the "better-than-average" effect, wherein there is a belief that one's opinion or judgment is as good as it could be, leading to blindness to their subjective biases.

One example of how this theory applies in real life can be seen in how people choose leaders and politicians. Individuals might recognize the potential biases, ranging from the perceived level of security provided to the promises of economic stability when considering the other candidates. Still, they might ignore the same regarding their preferred candidate.

QUESTIONS

1. Can you think of a situation in which you were unaware of your own bias while recognizing it in others? How

might this blind spot have affected your thoughts or actions?

2. How can becoming aware of your own blind spots help you improve your relationships and decision making?

3. What strategies can you use to regularly reflect on and recognize your own biases so you can address your blind spots?

COGNITIVE DISSONANCE THEORY

Cognitive Dissonance Theory, developed by Leon Festinger in 1957, proposes that individuals strive for internal consistency in their beliefs, opinions, and actions. When inconsistencies arise among these cognitions, it leads to psychological discomfort known as cognitive dissonance. To alleviate this discomfort, people are inclined to reduce the dissonance by altering their attitudes, beliefs, or behaviors.

For example, if someone experiences buyer's remorse after purchasing an expensive gadget, they might cope with this dissonance by justifying the purchase, focusing on the gadget's positive features, or convincing themselves of its necessity, thereby realigning their beliefs with their action and reducing the dissonance. Introduced in the late 1950s, this theory has been influential in understanding how individuals seek to maintain psychological consistency.

QUESTIONS:

1. Have you ever experienced cognitive dissonance in your relationships, perhaps after acting in a way that contradicts your beliefs? How did you resolve this?

2. In your career, how can awareness of cognitive dissonance aid in ethical decision-making and maintaining integrity?

3. What strategies can you employ to confront and reduce cognitive dissonance for personal growth and self-awareness?

CONFIRMATION BIAS

Peter Wason proposed the concept of confirmation bias in the 1960s.

Confirmation bias is the tendency of individuals to search for, interpret, favor, and recall information that confirms or strengthens their preexisting beliefs or hypotheses. Individuals and groups can display confirmation bias when gathering or interpreting evidence, making decisions, and forming memories. In doing so, they embrace and retain information supporting their beliefs while discounting information contradicting them.

An example of confirmation bias in action is the tendency of individuals to favor information that supports their current opinion while discounting evidence that contradicts it. For example, suppose one believes that a particular political candidate is the best option in an election. In that case, they may search for and focus on news sources and online outlets that reinforce their opinion, even if those sources are not necessarily credible or reliable.

QUESTIONS

1. Can you identify a situation in which you sought or focused on information that confirmed your existing

beliefs while disregarding contradictory evidence? How did this bias affect your view?

2. How can being aware of confirmation bias help you make more objective decisions and develop an open-minded attitude?

3. What practices can you use to actively challenge your beliefs and expose yourself to different perspectives to counteract bias?

FUNDAMENTAL ATTRIBUTION ERROR

The fundamental attribution error, also known as the correspondence bias, was first coined by social psychologist Lee Ross in 1977.

The fundamental attribution error is an error in thinking that assumes an individual's behavior reflects their inherent character rather than external factors. It is an example of a cognitive bias in which an individual tends to over-attribute behavior to a particular trait of that person rather than external circumstances.

For example, if a person is seen to be aggressive when driving, the fundamental attribution error would incorrectly imply that the driver is inherently aggressive and overlook other external factors, such as the environmental conditions or the driver's mental state.

QUESTIONS

1. How might fundamental attribution error affect your perception of the behavior of others in your personal or professional life?

2. Can you recall a situation in which you attributed a person's actions to their character rather than considering external factors? How would acknowledging the

basic attribution error change your understanding of the situation?

3. What steps can you take to consistently consider situational factors when interpreting the actions of others in order to avoid the basic attribution error?

HALO EFFECT

The Halo Effect is a cognitive bias first described by social psychologist Edward Thorndike in the 1920s. It describes the phenomenon where the perception of a particular trait in a person or entity influences our evaluation of other unrelated traits. To put it another way, we tend to let one trait or experience of a person, product, or company shape our overall judgment of that thing or person.

For example, if a company is known for financial stability, the organization might be seen more favorably regarding its customer service, even if it's spotty. Or, if a person is well educated, they may be perceived as more intelligent, even if they've done a poor job at an assignment. The Halo Effect has real-world implications for marketing, branding, and hiring practices.

QUESTIONS

1. Can you think of an instance in which the halo effect may have influenced your judgment of someone based on a single positive trait or experience?

2. How can recognizing the halo effect help you develop a more balanced and comprehensive understanding of people and situations?

3. What strategies can you use to counteract the halo effect and ensure that you judge people and situations based on multiple factors, not just a single positive trait?

HINDSIGHT BIAS

The founder of hindsight bias is Baruch Fischhoff, a cognitive scientist and social and decision sciences professor at Carnegie Mellon University.

This theory was first published in 1975 in an article published in the Journal of Personality and Social Psychology.

Hindsight bias is a cognitive bias that affects people's memory and perspective of past events. It manifests when people believe they have a sense of foresight regarding an event, even though they do not know it. This is also known as the "knew-it-all-along" effect.

Hindsight bias can cause people to overestimate their abilities to predict the outcome of a future event. For example, if one succeeds at a task such as picking a winning sports team, they will be more likely to believe that they already "knew" they were going to win, even though they were still unsure before the event took place.

QUESTIONS

1. How has bias in hindsight affected your perception of past events or decisions in your life? How might this bias affect your future decisions?

2. Can you name a situation in which you may have been a victim of hindsight bias? How can acknowledging this bias help you better understand your past decisions?

3. What practices can you adopt to minimize the influence of hindsight bias and maintain a balanced perspective when reflecting on past events or decisions?

ILLUSORY CORRELATION

Illusory correlation is a cognitive bias in which individuals perceive a correlation between two events that are not related. This concept was first put forward in 1979 by psychologist Leonard Berkowitz. Illusory correlation is especially prevalent when one notices a consequence and then assumes the preceding behavior is causative. In other words, it is when a relationship between two events is incorrectly perceived due to a prior association.

For example, a person wearing a white shirt assumes that if a person has been wearing a white shirt for a long time and something bad happens, they must have caused it by wearing the white shirt. This perception is illusory as the two events are unrelated and do not influence each other in any way whatsoever.

QUESTIONS

1. Can you recall a situation in which you perceived a relationship between two variables that did not actually exist? How did this illusory correlation affect your beliefs or actions?

2. How can being aware of illusory correlations help you make more objective judgments and decisions?

3. What strategies can you use to critically analyze relationships between variables and avoid falling into the trap of illusory correlations?

ILLUSORY SUPERIORITY

Illusory Superiority (also known as the Above Average Effect) is a cognitive bias that reflects an individual's overestimation of their abilities and qualities relative to the same qualities of others. The term was first coined by sociologist and professor of psychology David Dunning and Stanford professor and Social Psychologist Justin Kruger in 1999. This theory suggests that individuals are more likely to overestimate their talents, capabilities, and performance when compared to peers.

The theory suggests that people may form a false understanding of themselves because of the lack of accurate feedback and information. For example, someone may think they are above average at a certain skill, such as public speaking, when their skill level is the same as everyone else's.

Illusory Superiority can be seen in everyday life. For example, in a hypothetical scenario, three coworkers are tasked with cleaning their office space. They are all relatively new to the position and do not have any prior experience with cleaning. As a result, all three coworkers may think that they are performing the task better than their peers due to the lack of accurate feedback and could overestimate the quality of their work.

QUESTIONS

1. In what areas of your life have you experienced illusory superiority, that is, the belief that you are better than others or more capable than you actually are?

2. How can recognizing illusory superiority help you develop a more accurate self-assessment and promote personal growth?

3. What practices can you use to maintain a balanced and realistic assessment of your abilities to counteract illusory superiority?

NEGATIVITY BIAS

In a study by Alice H. Eagly and Shelly Chaiken, participants read descriptions of two hypothetical politicians, one with an equal number of positive and negative attributes and the other with a majority of positive attributes. Despite the equal overall evaluation of the two politicians, participants tended to rate the politician with a majority of positive attributes as less competent than the other politician.

This theory postulates that negative stimuli are more powerful than positive stimuli and carry greater weight when the individual is making decisions or judgments.

This theory is applicable in many situations in real life. For instance, in workplace activities, negativity bias can create a situation in which negative emotions are prioritized more than positive ones, leading to a lack of motivation and decreased performance.

QUESTIONS

1. Can you identify a situation in which a negative bias may have influenced your thoughts or decisions by focusing on negative information or experiences?

2. How can recognizing and understanding negativity help you cultivate a more balanced perspective on life?

3. What techniques can you use to counteract negative bias and develop a more positive perspective in your personal and professional life?

NEGATIVITY EFFECT

The Negativity Effect is the concept that people tend to overestimate the occurrence and effect of negative events and memories while underestimating the occurrence and effect of positive ones. Social psychologist Tom Bower first proposed and examined the concept in 1975.

It is theorized that the reasoning behind this phenomenon is that the human brain's response to threatening or potentially dangerous stimuli is stronger than its response to positive or neutral stimuli.

An example of this would be that people may remember negative interactions with a colleague more easily than positive ones and be more likely to react more strongly to resentful comments or situations in the workplace.

QUESTIONS

1. How has the negativity effect, the tendency to give more weight to negative experiences, affected your feelings or decisions in the past?

2. How can recognizing the negativity effect help you develop a more balanced and objective perspective when evaluating situations?

3. What strategies can you use to focus on the positive aspects of your life and counteract the negativity effect?

REPRESENTATIVENESS HEURISTIC

Amos Tversky and Daniel Kahneman introduced the representativeness heuristic.

The representativeness heuristic was first introduced in 1972.

The representativeness heuristic is a cognitive bias that relies on the appearance of similarities between an object and its context. This heuristic enables one to judge an object's characteristics, or an event's likelihood, based on how similar it appears to something else we already know. It can be used to estimate probabilities and to make decisions based on treatments of past occurrences.

For example, say you are presented with two boxes. One is filled with 100 coins, of which 75 are from one country, and the other 25 are from another. The second box is filled with 50 coins, of which 25 are from the same country (the first 75 coins come from), and the other 25 come from a different country. Using the representativeness heuristic, one is likely to assume that the first box contains more coins than the second, even though it is not true. In this instance, the first box appears to be 'more representative' of the original country.

QUESTIONS

1. How has the representativeness heuristic, the tendency to judge the likelihood of an event based on how similar it is to a prototype, influenced your decision making in the past?

2. How can awareness of the representativeness heuristic help you make more accurate judgments and decisions?

3. What strategies can you use to counteract the representativeness heuristic and consider a broader range of information when making probability judgments?

SELECTIVE PERCEPTION THEORY

Selective perception refers to the tendency of individuals to unconsciously filter out information that is inconsistent with their beliefs or values. In a study by Muzafer Sherif, participants were shown a dot of light in a dark room and asked to estimate its movement. Despite the light being stationary, participants reported that it moved in various directions, demonstrating the power of perceptual biases.

One example of selective perception in everyday life is how people process political messages. People tend to rely strongly on the news broadcasts they watch or read, so they become more closely aligned with the political party or candidate their preferred source tends to favor. As a result, they experience selective perception, with any opposing argument being overlooked or discredited.

QUESTIONS

1. Can you think of an instance where selective perception influenced your interpretation of an event or situation based on your pre-existing beliefs or expectations?

2. How can becoming aware of selective perception help you develop a more open and unbiased view of the world around you?

3. What practices can you use to actively challenge your selective perception and expose yourself to different perspectives and experiences?

SELF-ESTEEM BIAS

This bias is mainly attributed to the early twentieth-century psychologist William James, who suggested that people tend to believe that their opinions and those closest to them are superior to those of others. An example of this bias in the real world would be the "tall poppy syndrome," where equally skilled and talented individuals are not given the same opportunities because one individual is perceived as better than the others. As a result, this individual is given greater recognition and opportunities at the expense of the rest. This thought process can create envy, anger, and disappointment in those who have been overlooked, leading to further prejudice and discrimination.

QUESTIONS

1. Can you name a situation in which self-esteem bias may have influenced your perception of yourself or others? How did this bias affect your thinking or actions?

2. How can being aware of self-esteem bias help you develop a more balanced and accurate self-assessment and understanding of others?

3. What strategies can you use to deal with self-esteem issues and promote a healthy self-image that accurately reflects your abilities and accomplishments?

SELF-SERVING BIAS

In the 1970s, David L. Rosenhan put forward this theory. It states that people perceive their opinions and decisions positively. They take credit for their successes while attributing their failures to external factors.

The Self-Serving Bias theory can be applied to various aspects of life. For example, a student who got an A+ in Math class will likely claim that the result was due to their sheer hard work and discipline while attributing other lower grades to other factors such as the professor not being clear enough or the subject being too difficult.

This type of behavior is very common in modern society. This theory emphasizes how that kind of behavior can lead to negative consequences, such as overconfidence in situations where individuals are likely to underperform and an inability to accept criticism even when it's justified.

QUESTIONS

1. Can you think of a situation in which you attributed your successes to your own abilities and efforts, while blaming external factors for your failures? How did this self-serving bias affect your perception of yourself?

2. How can recognizing self-serving biases help you take responsibility for your successes and failures and promote personal growth?

3. What practices can you use to maintain a balanced and objective view of your actions and outcomes to counteract self-serving bias?

SOCIAL COMPARISON BIAS

Psychologist Leon Festinger established this theory in 1954. It suggests that when people are uncertain of their ability or opinion, they rely on others when it comes to self-evaluation. People develop their self-evaluation based on how they compare to others who seem similar to them. An example of this is when two students are given the same task to complete in the same amount of time. Suppose one student completes the task in less time. In that case, the other student might compare themselves to them — and their self-evaluation of the performance will likely be lower due to the comparison to a perceived equal, who appears to have done better.

QUESTIONS

1. How has social comparison, the process of assessing yourself in comparison to others, affected your personal growth, relationships, and experiences?

2. How can understanding social comparison theory help you recognize and address the potential impact of social comparison on your thoughts, feelings, and behaviors?

3. What strategies can you use to minimize the negative effects of social comparison and promote a self-compassionate and growth mindset?

TRIARCHIC THEORY OF INTELLIGENCE

Psychologist Robert Sternberg developed the Triarchic Theory of Intelligence in the 1980s and 1990s.

This theory proposes that intelligence can be divided into three main components: analytical intelligence, creative intelligence, and practical intelligence.

Analytical intelligence involves analyzing and evaluating information and solving problems using logical and analytical thinking.

An example of this theory in action might be seen in a business setting. An entrepreneur with strong analytical intelligence might be able to analyze financial data and identify areas where cost savings can be achieved. However, lacking creative intelligence, they may struggle to develop new and innovative business growth ideas. Similarly, if they lack practical intelligence, they may struggle to adapt to changing market conditions or to effectively manage their employees.

QUESTIONS

1. According to Sternberg's triarchic theory of intelligence, intelligence is composed of an analytical dimension, a creative dimension, and a practical dimension. Which

of these dimensions do you think are your strengths, and which do you need to develop further?

2. How can understanding the triarchic theory of intelligence help you recognize the potential impact of different dimensions of intelligence on your relationships, personal growth, and career success?

3. What strategies can you implement to cultivate and enhance your different analytical, creative, and practical intelligence, fostering an adaptable approach to decision-making in your life?

PERSONALITY AND DEVELOPMENT THEORIES

ACCEPTANCE AND COMMITMENT THERAPY (ACT) PRINCIPLES

Developed in the late 20th century by psychologist Steven C. Hayes, Acceptance and Commitment Therapy (ACT) is a form of psychotherapy that integrates mindfulness strategies with behavioral change. This approach is rooted in the belief that psychological suffering is often caused by trying to avoid or control emotional experiences, and instead emphasizes accepting these experiences while committing to action based on personal values.

ACT is built on six core processes: Cognitive Defusion, Acceptance, Contact with the Present Moment, Observing the Self, Values, and Committed Action. For example, in the context of workplace stress, ACT would encourage an individual not to avoid or deny feelings of anxiety but rather to accept them as part of the human experience. Simultaneously, it would guide them to clarify their core values (like personal growth or teamwork) and take actions aligned with these values, despite the presence of stress or anxiety.

One key aspect of ACT is the concept of 'psychological flexibility,' which is the ability to be in the present moment more fully and to change or persist in behavior that is aligned with one's values. This approach helps individuals to embrace their thoughts and feelings rather than fighting them, finding ways to live a rich and meaningful life in spite of the inevitable pains and struggles. ACT has been applied effectively to a wide range of issues from anxiety to chronic pain, emphasizing a life led in accordance with one's values as the key to true psychological health.

QUESTIONS:

1. How can embracing the principles of Acceptance and Commitment Therapy (ACT) enhance your personal relationships, particularly by practicing acceptance and

mindfulness in understanding and communicating your feelings and needs?

2. In what ways can applying ACT's core processes, such as defining your values and committed action, influence your approach to career development and workplace challenges, especially when considering decisions that reflect what truly matters to you?

3. What strategies from ACT can you implement to deal with life's difficulties more effectively, considering that developing psychological flexibility can help you accept your thoughts and feelings and act in alignment with your values?

ADLERIAN THEORY

Adlerian Theory is a personality theory developed by founder Alfred Adler (1870-1937).

This theory summarizes that when people feel a lack of significance and self-worth, they will strive to make up for it by pursuing superiority through their actions or thought.

A real-life example of this theory is when a person feels a lack of self-worth or significance and then decides to become better through gaining knowledge or success. They can do this by choosing a career or working on completing school, either of which acts as a way to gain status and superiority. This feeling of importance can then lead to other positive outcomes, such as improved self-esteem and better relationships.

QUESTIONS

1. How do the concepts of inferiority and superiority complexes impact your personal and professional life? How do these complexes affect your relationships and self-esteem?

2. In what ways are you striving for personal growth and self-improvement as emphasized in Adlerian theory? How can understanding this theory enhance your personal development?

3. How can you apply the concept of "social interest" from Adlerian theory to build stronger, more empathetic relationships with others in your life?

ATTACHMENT THEORY

John Bowlby established the Attachment Theory in the mid-20th century.

The theory suggests that early experiences with caregivers, particularly in the first years of life, shape an individual's attachment style, affecting their social and emotional development. According to Bowlby, a secure attachment bond with a caregiver promotes feelings of safety and security and sets the stage for healthy relationships in adulthood. An example of this theory in action might be seen in a child who is securely attached to their caregiver. The child is comfortable exploring their environment and interacting with others, knowing that their caregiver is a source of safety and comfort when needed. As the child grows up, they are likely to develop healthy relationships with others based on trust and emotional security. Conversely, an insecurely attached child can struggle to form healthy relationships later in life, experiencing difficulty with intimacy and trust. Attachment theory has been widely applied in clinical settings to help individuals improve their relationships and develop greater emotional security.

QUESTIONS

1. How would you describe your attachment style, and how has it affected your relationships and interactions with others?

2. How can understanding attachment theory help you build stronger and healthier relationships with friends, family, and romantic partners?

3. What steps can you take to promote secure attachments in your current and future relationships based on attachment theory?

BEHAVIORAL THEORY

This psychological approach to understanding human behavior was originally proposed by John B. Watson, a renowned American psychologist.

This theory summarizes that all behaviors are shaped by the environment and can be changed through interventions and behavior modification.

A real-life example of this theory is when an individual stops doing an unwanted behavior in response to a negative consequence. For example, suppose an individual often gets into trouble in school for talking during class. In that case, they may respond to the punishment of being sent outside for the remainder of the period by refraining from talking and instead participating in class. In this case, the unwanted behavior of talking was curbed due to negative consequences. Behaviorism emphasizes that behaviors are shaped by what happens in response to them and provides various strategies to manage unwanted ones.

QUESTIONS

1. Can you identify learned behaviors in your life that have been shaped by reinforcement or punishment? How

have these behaviors impacted your personal and professional experiences?

2. How can understanding behavioral theory help you change or replace unhelpful learned behaviors and develop new, positive habits?

3. What strategies can you use to apply the principles of behavioral theory in your daily life to enhance your personal growth and improve your relationships with others?

CONSTRUCTIVIST THEORY

Jean Piaget and Lev Vygotsky established the Constructivist Theory in 1936. This theory summarizes that learning occurs when students construct their knowledge. Students should explore and interact with the world around them, as problem-solving, exploration, and discovery all lead to the formation of new knowledge. This theory encourages the idea that teachers should be more facilitators than lecturers. A real-life example of this theory is project-based learning. This form of learning allows students to engage in an activity that requires problem-solving and critical thinking, which allows them to absorb new knowledge and better understand the material. Ultimately, the constructivist theory of learning advocates that the individual generates knowledge through experience and understanding.

QUESTIONS

1. How has your personal construction system, i.e., the unique mental constructs you use to interpret and make sense of the world, influenced your thoughts, feelings, and actions?

2. How can understanding constructivist theory help you identify and address unhelpful or limiting constructs in your life?

3. What strategies can you use to actively reshape your personal construct system in ways that promote personal growth and adaptability?

52

DEVELOPMENTAL THEORY

Developmental theory is a broad set of theories about developing a person's identity, relationships, and social environment. It is a broad concept that encapsulates a variety of theories about the stages of human development. Its founder, Jean Piaget, first outlined the theory as "the transition from a state of innocence to a state of knowledge." Piaget developed four distinct stages of development.

Those stages are:

- Sensorimotor Stage: 0 – 2 years
- Preoperational Stage: 2 – 7 years
- Concrete Operational Stage: 7 – 11 years
- Formal Operational Stage: 12+ years

A real-life example of this theory is a child learning how to stand, walk, or talk. Development progresses as people age through the process of maturation as well as social and environmental influences. Another example is a teenager transitioning into adulthood and gaining independence by attending college or getting a job. Through these experiences, the individual can form an identity, learn how to interact with others, and become a more productive individual in society.

QUESTIONS

1. Can you identify specific developmental stages or periods in your life that have had a significant impact on your personal growth and identity?

2. How can understanding developmental theory help you understand the ongoing process of personal growth and change throughout your life?

3. What practices can you use to support your ongoing development and overcome challenges or transitions associated with different life stages?

DIALECTICAL BEHAVIOR THERAPY (DBT)

Dialectical Behavior Therapy (DBT), developed by psychologist Marsha M. Linehan in the late 20th century, is a comprehensive cognitive-behavioral treatment that emphasizes the psychosocial aspects of therapy. DBT was initially designed to treat individuals with borderline personality disorder and chronic suicidal ideation. It has since been adapted for a variety of other conditions, including eating disorders, substance use disorders, and depression.

The core principle of DBT is the balance between acceptance and change. It combines standard cognitive-behavioral techniques for emotional regulation and reality-testing with concepts of distress tolerance, acceptance, and mindful awareness largely derived from Buddhist meditative practice. For example, a person undergoing DBT might learn skills to tolerate painful emotions in a healthy way and to improve relationships through assertiveness and empathy.

DBT is structured around four main components: mindfulness, distress tolerance, emotion regulation, and interpersonal effectiveness. In practical terms, this might involve learning to be fully present in the moment, managing difficult emotional states without resorting to self-destructive behaviors, regulating emotions to reduce impulsivity, and navigating interpersonal relationships more effectively.

This therapy is unique in its focus on the synthesis of opposites as a cornerstone of its philosophy and practice - the dialectical component. DBT teaches skills to help individuals develop a life that feels worth living, emphasizing both acceptance and change to bring about positive improvements in mental health and overall well-being.

QUESTIONS:

1. Considering DBT's emphasis on balancing acceptance and change, how can applying these principles to your personal relationships enhance your ability to manage conflicts and deepen connections with empathy and understanding?

2. In the context of your career, how can DBT skills like mindfulness, distress tolerance, emotion regulation, and interpersonal effectiveness contribute to a more productive and less stressful work environment?

3. What steps can you take to integrate DBT principles into your personal growth strategy, particularly in developing a more balanced approach to accepting challenges while actively working towards change?

DISPOSITIONAL THEORY

Psychologist Raymond Cattell established it in the 1930s.

This theory summarizes that each person's behavior is determined by their underlying trait structure, meaning that people have certain inborn predispositions and tendencies that influence how they act in certain situations. Ultimately, these traits, or dispositions, dictate how they respond to and interact with the world around them.

A real-life example of this theory is people with a naturally optimistic disposition—they approach life positively. As a result, they are more likely to move through difficult times with hope and happiness. In contrast, those with a less optimistic disposition may struggle more with negative emotions. Similarly, those with a more outgoing disposition may be more likely to thrive in social gatherings, while their more introspective peers may find social situations daunting.

QUESTIONS

1. How do your dispositional traits, stable characteristics that influence your thinking and behavior, shape your interactions with others and your overall outlook on life?

2. How can understanding dispositional theory help you recognize and use your unique characteristics to enhance your personal development and improve your relationships?

3. What strategies can you use to manage or adjust your dispositional traits to live a more balanced and fulfilling life?

ECOLOGICAL SYSTEMS THEORY

Psychologist Urie Bronfenbrenner developed ecological Systems Theory (Bioecological Theory) in the 1970s.

The theory suggests that an individual's development is influenced by a complex system of interactions between the individual and their environment, which can be divided into four different systems: the microsystem, mesosystem, ecosystem, and macrosystem.

An example of this theory in action might be seen in a child struggling in school. An Ecological Systems perspective would examine not only the child's characteristics but also their relationships with their family, peers, and teachers (microsystem), the connections between these different aspects of their life (mesosystem), the institutional policies and resources available to support their education (ecosystem), and the cultural beliefs and values that shape their expectations and experiences (macrosystem). This perspective can help identify the factors contributing to the child's difficulties and inform interventions that target multiple levels of their environment.

QUESTIONS

1. How have the various systems (microsystem, mesosystem, exosystem, macrosystem, and chronosystem) in your life affected your personal growth and experiences?

2. How can understanding ecological systems theory help you identify and address the various environmental factors that impact your well-being and relationships?

3. What strategies can you use to promote positive change within the various systems that influence your life to achieve personal growth and well-being?

HUMANISTIC THEORY

The Humanistic Theory is a school of thought developed by the founder, Carl Rogers. This theory summarizes that human behavior is largely based upon the belief in self-worth, which is determined by a person's understanding of their environment, circumstances, and experiences. Therefore, people who accept their worth and experiences in life are more inclined to be self-motivated and develop stronger interpersonal relationships with those around them.

A real-life example of this theory is seen in the lives of students who study hard and do their best to get ahead. If a student can recognize their worth, they will be more motivated to do well and strive to achieve more in life.

QUESTIONS

1. In what ways have you experienced self-actualization or the realization of your full potential in your personal and professional life?

2. How can understanding humanistic theory help you identify and remove obstacles to self-actualization and enhance your personal growth?

3. What practices can you adopt to promote self-actualization and develop a more authentic, fulfilling life based on the principles of humanistic theory?

62

LOGOTHERAPY

Logotherapy, developed by psychiatrist and holocaust survivor Viktor Frankl in the mid-20th century, is a form of psychotherapy that emphasizes the search for meaning in life as the primary human drive. Frankl's experiences in concentration camps during World War II profoundly shaped his understanding of human psychology and the importance of finding purpose, even in the most dire circumstances.

The central tenet of Logotherapy is that a fundamental pursuit of meaning, rather than a pursuit of pleasure or power, is what motivates human beings. For instance, in the face of a life-altering event such as a severe illness, Logotherapy suggests that finding personal meaning in this experience can be a source of strength. It encourages individuals to see challenging experiences not as obstacles, but as opportunities to find purpose and direction.

Logotherapy introduces several concepts, including the "will to meaning," "existential frustration," and "existential vacuum." Frankl's therapy focuses on helping individuals identify and pursue meaningful life goals and to find meaning in suffering if necessary. This approach is known for its applications in helping people cope with severe stress and trauma, and in fostering resilience. It empowers individuals to live with a sense of purpose and fulfillment, even in the face of life's inevitable challenges.

QUESTIONS:

1. How can integrating the principles of Logotherapy into your personal relationships help deepen connections by fostering a shared pursuit of meaningful goals and understanding each other's search for purpose?

2. Considering Logotherapy's emphasis on finding personal meaning in all life's circumstances, how can this perspective influence your career path and response to professional setbacks or challenges?

3. What steps can you take to apply Logotherapy's concepts in your everyday life, particularly in using existential challenges as opportunities to discover and pursue meaningful objectives?

MEADOW MAPPING: A HOLISTIC APPROACH TO EVOLUTION

Meadow Mapping, conceptualized by Nils von Heijne and Amit Paul, is a theory that draws inspiration from the cyclical nature of life. This theory outlines a transformative approach for individuals, communities, and organizations to understand and navigate their evolutionary journeys.

By recognizing five distinct phases – Seeding, Sprouting, Blooming, Withering, and Composting – Meadow Mapping offers a framework for understanding growth, maturity, and renewal. Each phase represents a critical step in the cycle of evolution, emphasizing the importance of acknowledging and embracing each for holistic development. For instance, an individual may explore various aspects of their lives (e.g. their evolution of identity, interests, relationships, work, thought patterns, emotional challenges etc.) by noting what is currently seeding, sprouting, blooming, withering and composting. This cycle mirrors the natural processes observed in ecosystems, underscoring the interconnectedness of all life forms and their growth patterns. It can be applied to any evolutionary process in individuals, relationships, groups, communities, nations etc. – and as such it offers a meta approach to any inner development or coaching context.

QUESTIONS:

1. Reflect on a relevant realm of your life: can you identify the various phases of Meadow Mapping and what is defining each phase at the moment?

2. How can recognizing the phases you're in assist in making more informed decisions and preparing for your continued journey?

3. What strategies can you implement to honor what is needed in each phase and navigate from one phase to another more smoothly, ensuring your continuous evolution and adaptation?

Meadow Mapping challenges the traditional linear perspective on growth and success, advocating for a more nuanced understanding that embraces the natural ebbs and flows of life's journey. This theory is particularly relevant in a world that values constant innovation and adaptation, offering a compassionate lens through which we can view ourselves and our impact on the world around us.

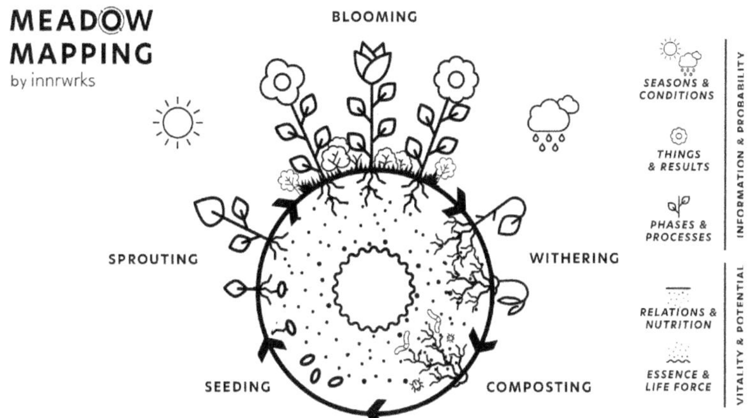
MEADOW
MAPPING
by innrwrks
BLOOMING
SPROUTING
WITHERING
SEEDING
COMPOSTING
SEASONS &
CONDITIONS
THINGS
& RESULTS
PHASES &
PROCESSES
RELATIONS &
NUTRITION
ESSENCE &
LIFE FORCE
INFORMATION & PROBABILITY
VITALITY & POTENTIAL

OBJECT RELATIONS THEORY

Object Relations Theory, significantly influenced by psychoanalyst Melanie Klein in the mid-20th century, provides a framework for understanding human psyche through the lens of interpersonal relationships. This theory posits that our psychological processes are deeply influenced by our early relationships, primarily those with primary caregivers.

The essence of Object Relations Theory lies in the belief that our earliest experiences of attachment, and the images we form of ourselves and others based on these experiences, fundamentally shape our future interpersonal dynamics and sense of self. For example, a child who experiences nurturing and secure relationships with caregivers is likely to develop a healthy, integrated sense of self and the ability to form positive relationships in adulthood.

Klein's work, along with other contributors to this theory, emphasizes the importance of early emotional attachments and how they contribute to the formation of an internal 'object world' - a mental representation of oneself and others. This inner world influences an individual's behavior and emotional experiences throughout their life.

In practical applications, such as therapy, Object Relations Theory can help individuals understand and resolve issues rooted in their early relationships. It offers insights into how past experiences shape current behavior and emotional responses, and how modifying these internalized object relations can lead to psychological healing and growth.

The theory is particularly valuable for exploring issues related to attachment, identity, and interpersonal relationships, providing a deep understanding of how early experiences influence adult life.

QUESTIONS:

1. How can understanding the principles of Object Relations Theory enhance your approach to personal relationships, especially by recognizing how early attachments might influence your current relationship dynamics?

2. In what ways can integrating Object Relations Theory into your professional interactions help you address and mitigate potential conflicts or misunderstandings, considering the impact of your internal 'object world' on these dynamics?

3. What steps can you take to use Object Relations Theory as a tool for personal development, particularly in exploring and healing from the effects of early relational experiences on your sense of self and your ability to form healthy adult relationships?

PSYCHOANALYSIS THEORY

The renowned Austrian neurologist and psychiatrist Sigmund Freud developed Psychoanalysis Theory.

Freud believed that most of our behavior and emotional states are based on conflicts in our unconscious mind. He argued that our behavior could be explained by conflict between the id, ego, and superego. The id consists of our impulses and primitive urges, the ego is our rational self, and the superego consists of moral values and ideals. Thus, our ego struggles to balance between these forces.

Real-life examples of this theory can be seen in how we deal with our relationships. How we respond in a situation will depend on many factors, namely, our relationship history, upbringing, experiences, etc. For example, if a person has a history of bad relationships, then they may respond defensively in their current relationship to protect themselves from heartbreak.

QUESTIONS

1. Can you identify recurring themes, patterns, or conflicts in your thoughts, feelings, and behaviors that may be related to unconscious processes?

2. How can understanding psychoanalytic theory help you gain insight into unconscious influences on your personal growth, relationships, and well-being?

3. What techniques or practices can you use to explore and address unconscious influences and promote greater self-knowledge and personal growth?

PSYCHOANALYTIC SOCIAL THEORY

The seminal work of psychoanalyst Erik Erikson established psychoanalytic Social Theory.

Psychoanalytic Social Theory is centered around the idea that psychological development occurs in various stages, which can influence an individual's social experience. This theory suggests that, by actively engaging with others, all individuals will go through different stages of development and learning to become mature, well-rounded, and successful adults.

An example of applying this theory can be seen in childcare settings. Many childcare providers and teachers use methods of administering guidance and discipline influenced by Erik Erikson's psychoanalytic social theory. Since Erikson believed that the dynamics between people impacted an individual's development and maturation, childcare providers seek to foster an environment that encourages young children to explore their place in a social environment and gain new perspectives on the world around them.

QUESTIONS

1. How have social and cultural factors influenced the development of your personality according to psychoanalytic social theory?

2. How can understanding psychoanalytic social theory help you recognize the impact of social and cultural influences on your personal growth and relationships?

3. What strategies can you use to combat unfavorable social or cultural influences on your life and promote better self-knowledge and personal development?

PSYCHODYNAMIC THEORY

Sigmund Freud, the father of psychoanalysis, established the psychodynamic theory.

This theory summarizes that the dynamic interactions of our psyche greatly influence our lives and how we act.

A real-life example of this theory could be seen in a child's behavior. A child may have a constant need for approval. This is the influence of the id (pleasure-seeking) on the child's behavior. The child's ego may recognize the reality of wanting approval and attempt to control the child's behavior according to this reality, provided the child's superego allows them to behave in this way. If the child's superego holds strict values, they may try to act in a certain way to gain approval while also trying to act according to the values in the child's superego. In this way, the three parts of the psyche constantly interact, influencing each other to result in the child's behaviors.

QUESTIONS

1. Can you identify unconscious mental processes or unresolved conflicts that psychodynamic theory suggests influence your thoughts, feelings, and behaviors?

2. How can understanding psychodynamic theory help you gain insight into the underlying factors that influence your personal growth, relationships, and well-being?

3. What techniques or practices can you use to explore and address unconscious influences and promote greater self-knowledge and personal growth based on the principles of psychodynamic theory?

RESILIENCE THEORY

Resilience Theory, a concept extensively studied and developed by various psychologists, delves into the dynamic process enabling individuals to adapt, recover, and thrive amidst adversity, stress, or trauma. This theory posits that resilience is not an inherent trait but rather a capacity that can be cultivated and enhanced over time through various experiences and strategies.

One real-life example of resilience is an individual bouncing back from a significant setback, such as job loss or the passing of a loved one. Instead of being permanently overwhelmed by the situation, they find ways to adapt positively, perhaps by exploring new career paths, redefining personal goals, or strengthening social connections. This ability to recover and even grow in the wake of challenges is central to the concept of resilience. The theory underscores the role of environmental factors, personal resources, and learned coping strategies in building and sustaining resilience, suggesting it's a dynamic and evolving process rather than a static trait.

QUESTIONS:

1. Can you recall a time when you faced a significant challenge or setback? How did you adapt and what did you learn about your resilience?

2. In your career, how can understanding and fostering resilience help you deal with professional setbacks or changes?

3. What practices or habits can you adopt to build resilience and support your personal growth and well-being?

ROGERS' PERSON-CENTERED THEORY

Carl Rogers established Person-Centered Theory, also known as Client-Centered Therapy, which he developed in the mid-20th century.

The theory suggests that individuals have an inherent capacity for growth and self-actualization. This potential can be realized through a therapeutic relationship characterized by empathy, unconditional positive regard, and congruence.

Rogers believed that individuals have a natural inclination towards personal growth and that this growth is inhibited by external forces such as societal expectations and the opinions of others. An example of this theory in action might be seen in a person struggling with anxiety. With person-centered therapy, a therapist might work with the individual to identify the underlying causes of their anxiety and help them develop strategies for coping with these feelings. The therapist would provide a safe and supportive environment where individuals can explore their thoughts and feelings without fear of judgment or criticism. By fostering a sense of acceptance and understanding, the therapist can help the individual move towards self-acceptance and personal growth.

QUESTIONS

1. How do you experience and express empathy, unconditional positive regard, and sincerity in your relationships with others, according to Rogers' person-centered theory?

2. How can understanding person-centered theory help you build stronger relationships with others and promote personal growth through authenticity and acceptance?

3. What practices can you use to cultivate a person-centered approach in your relationships and interactions to support your own personal growth and the well-being of others?

SELF-COMPASSION

Self-Compassion, as conceptualized by Kristin Neff, is a personal attribute that involves being kind and understanding towards oneself in instances of pain or failure, rather than being harshly self-critical. This theory, emerging in the early 2000s, underscores the importance of treating oneself with the same kindness and understanding one would offer to a good friend

This concept posits that self-compassion involves three main components: self-kindness, common humanity, and mindfulness. Individuals practicing self-compassion recognize that suffering and feelings of inadequacy are part of the human experience, allowing them to maintain a balanced perspective on their situation. For example, a person may fail at a professional task and, instead of self-flagellation, they might acknowledge their disappointment while also understanding that failure is a common human experience.

Self-compassion is shown to have a significant positive impact on mental well-being. It helps in reducing anxiety, depression, and stress. It encourages people to acknowledge their faults and failures without judgment or self-blame. This approach can be particularly beneficial when dealing with personal shortcomings or challenging life events, as it promotes emotional resilience and a more compassionate self-view.

QUESTIONS:

1. How can practicing self-compassion in personal relationships help you navigate and recover from conflicts more effectively, considering that being kind to yourself can lead to healthier communication and more empathetic interactions?

2. In what ways can integrating self-compassion into your professional life enhance your response to criticism or failure, given that self-kindness fosters resilience, enabling you to learn from feedback without self-doubt?

3. What steps can you take to cultivate self-compassion as a daily practice to promote your general growth and well-being, especially when acknowledging common humanity and practicing mindfulness can balance your perspective, encouraging growth?

SOCIAL COGNITIVE DEVELOPMENT THEORY

The social cognitive development theory by Jean Piaget was developed through observation and interviews with children of various ages. Piaget identified different stages of cognitive development, including the preoperational stage, where children are unable to understand conservation, and the concrete operational stage, where they begin to understand concepts like reversibility and conservation. His theory highlights the importance of cognitive development in shaping social behavior.

An example of how the Social Cognitive Development Theory can be applied in real life is through its longitudinal analysis of child development. This theory examines how children learn by observing, imitating, and understanding their environment. By understanding and applying the Social Cognitive Development Theory, professionals and parents can better understand how to foster a supportive and instructive environment for children. By observing and processing their environment, children learn to develop their own beliefs and behaviors, as well as how to interact with other individuals and objects. Understanding the Social Cognitive Development Theory creates interventions to help children learn how to make thoughtful and meaningful decisions.

QUESTIONS

1. How has your social cognitive development, or the way you learn and process information about others and the social world, influenced your personal growth and relationships?

2. How can understanding social cognitive development theory help you identify and address gaps or biases in your social understanding and decision making?

3. What strategies can you use to enhance your social cognitive development and improve your ability to navigate complex social situations and relationships?

SYSTEMS THEORY

Systems Theory is a transdisciplinary study that originates from the work of Ludwig von Bertalanffy, the founder of modern systems theory. Basically, any given system is a combination of interdependent components that work together to produce a certain outcome or set of conditions. Systems theory looks at not only the components of the outcomes but the dynamic interconnections between those components.

A real-life example of this theory can be seen in terms of a family unit. In this case, each family member is a component that works to produce the overall outcome of the family system. It is not only the individual that matters in this case, but also their relationships with one another that have an effect on the overall family dynamics. The family system has internal and external influences that can change the individuals in the family and the family as a whole.

QUESTIONS

1. How have various interconnected systems in your life, such as family, work, and social networks, affected your personal growth and well-being?

2. How can an understanding of systems theory help you identify and manage the complex dynamics and feed-back loops within these interconnected systems?

3. What strategies can you use to positively change the various systems in your life to enhance your personal growth and overall well-being?

THE ACTOR-PARTNER INTERDEPENDENCE MODEL

Kelley and Thibaut first proposed the actor-partner interdependence model in 1978. This model suggests that one partner's behavior in a relationship is influenced by both their own behavior and their partner's behavior. The model has been used to study relationships, including romantic and business partnerships.

In a romantic relationship, one partner's behavior may be influenced by their feelings and desires and their partner's behavior. If one partner is consistently late for dates, the other partner can feel less valued and may even start to question the relationship.

QUESTIONS

1. How have your thoughts, emotions, and behaviors influenced those of your close partners and vice versa, according to the Actor-Partner Interdependence Model?

2. How can understanding the Actor-Partner Interdependence Model help you recognize the reciprocal nature of close relationships and promote healthier, more balanced relationships?

3. What strategies can you use to address the interdependence between you and your close partners to promote mutual growth and well-being?

THE SELF-FULFILLING PROPHECY

The self-fulfilling prophecy is a phenomenon where a person's expectations about a situation or another person lead to behaviors that make those expectations come true. The original study by Rosenthal and Jacobson involved teachers who were given false information about the intelligence of certain students. Results showed that the teachers' expectations of the students' intelligence influenced their behavior towards them, resulting in higher academic performance by students labeled as "gifted." This study demonstrated how expectations could influence behavior and outcomes.

An example of this theory can be seen in the workplace. If a manager expects an employee to fail, they may subconsciously treat them as incompetent or criticize their work, leading the employee to fail.

QUESTIONS

1. Are there instances in your life where a self-fulfilling prophecy or the phenomenon of expectations influencing outcomes has occurred?

2. How can understanding the self-fulfilling prophecy help you recognize the power of your own beliefs and expectations to shape your experiences?

3. What strategies can you use to promote more positive,
    constructive self-fulfilling prophecy in your personal
    and professional life?

TRAIT THEORY

Trait Theory is a psychological theory originally developed by founder Gordon Allport. This theory posits that individual traits, or predispositions, are the basis of human behavior. It suggests that people differ in terms of their traits, and these differences largely explain behavior.

An example of a real-life application of Trait Theory is seen in the use of personality tests. Personality tests are used to measure psychological traits and characteristics that are believed to be significantly related to behavior and performance. For example, such tests typically demonstrate consistent correlations between traits such as agreeableness, openness to experience, conscientiousness, extraversion, and an individual's behavior. With the help of these tests, psychologists can gain insight into how individuals think and act and how these traits influence performance.

QUESTIONS

1. Can you identify your key personality traits and how they have influenced your personal growth, relationships, and experiences throughout your life?

2. How can understanding trait theory help you leverage your unique strengths and overcome challenges related to your personality traits?

3. What strategies can you use to develop a more balanced and adaptive approach to life based on the principles of trait theory?

SOCIAL AND CULTURAL THEORIES

ACCULTURATION THEORY

This is an approach to understanding the process of change that occurs when two different cultural groups come into contact with each other. It was developed by noted Harvard anthropologist Alfred Kroeber in 1948 and has been widely used in sociology, psychology, and linguistics.

At its core, it states that cultural change happens when an individual or group of individuals come into contact with a population that is culturally distinct from them. In such encounters, the less dominant culture is likely to adapt to the more dominant one, as the more dominant culture has more influence than the less dominant one. This adaptation often occurs in the form of language, values, and behaviors that align with the more dominant culture.

In real life, acculturation theory can play out in various contexts. One example could be a family who emigrates to a foreign country – the parents and the children might adopt the native language and values while keeping cultural practices and customs from the homeland. Another example could be mixing a dominant culture with a subculture or minority culture. The minority culture is often forced to take on the dominant one's values, beliefs, and behaviors as they are outnumbered and lack political power.

QUESTIONS

1. How has the process of acculturation, i.e., adapting to a new cultural environment, affected your personal growth, identity, and relationships?

2. How can understanding acculturation theory help you navigate the challenges and opportunities associated with cultural adaptation and change?

3. What strategies can you use to support a successful acculturation process and promote well-being during cultural transitions?

IMPLICIT BIAS THEORY

The Implicit Bias Theory was published in 1998 by Harvard psychologists Anthony G. Greenwald and Mahzarin Banaji. The theory states that individuals hold unconscious beliefs, preferences, and attitudes toward others based on race, gender, and age. This means people form and act on these implicit biases even when unaware. These biases can influence decisions and behaviors in various ways, including workplace policies, hiring practices, and how people interact with each other.

For example, implicit bias can manifest in identifying qualified job applicants, leading employers to overlook qualified individuals from certain backgrounds due to a pre-existing unconscious bias. In such scenarios, employers may select applicants based on shared experiences, knowledge or other factors that do not necessarily reflect the individual's qualifications.

QUESTIONS

1. Can you identify instances where implicit biases or unconscious attitudes or stereotypes have influenced your thoughts, feelings, or behaviors?

2. How can understanding implicit bias theory help you identify and address unconscious bias that can impact your personal growth and relationships?

3. What strategies can you use to challenge and reduce im-
    plicit bias to promote greater self-awareness, inclusivity,
    and personal growth?

EQUITY THEORY

The Equity Theory, developed in the late 1960s by social psychologist professor John Stacey Adams, attempts to explain why employees invest time and effort in their job and how this relates to the motivation of accomplishments in their work. This theory summarizes that employees will be motivated to work if they feel that their input and contributions (or perceived inputs and contributions) receive a "fair" output regarding reward or recognition.

For example, if an employee puts a significant amount of effort into completing a task and their rewards are commensurate with the effort they have put in, they will likely be motivated to maintain their current levels of effort. However, they will likely be demotivated if their perceived effort does not match their perceived reward.

QUESTIONS

1. How has the concept of equity or fairness and balance in relationships impacted your personal and professional relationships?

2. How can understanding equity theory help you identify and address imbalances or areas of dissatisfaction in your relationships?

3. What strategies can you use based on equity theory to promote greater equality and mutual satisfaction in your relationships?

IN-GROUP BIAS THEORY

In-Group Bias Theory, also known as 'in-group loyalty,' is a theory in social psychology first published in 1954 by the founding authors Muzafer Sherif and Carl Hovland. It is based on the idea that individuals tend to show preferential treatment toward their in-group compared to out-groups. The theory explains the psychological basis of individuals' attitudes, behaviors, and perceptions regarding their social environment.

On an individual level, an example of in-group bias theory in action can be seen when a person shows a more positive attitude towards their friends or family members and is less critical of their actions than strangers. For example, a person might have a negative attitude towards someone from a different cultural background due to the in-group bias theory. However, they might also show preferential behavior regarding privileges and opportunities for their in-group, such as providing more resources for their own family.

In a larger context, the theory explains phenomena such as racism, sexism, and other forms of bias in politics, the workplace, and other areas of society. The theory suggests the idea of an 'us' versus 'them' mentality that leads to discrimination and a sense of tribalism between in-groups and out-groups. It has been used to explain how some people gain more power or privileges in different situations due to their in-group's status in society.

QUESTIONS

1. Can you give examples from your life in which in-group bias, or the tendency to favor one's own group over others, has influenced your thoughts, feelings, or behaviors?

2. How can understanding the theory of in-group bias help you recognize and address the potential impact of this bias on your relationships and interactions with others?

3. What strategies can you use to address in-group bias and promote greater inclusivity, empathy, and understanding across groups?

INTERACTIONIST THEORY

Interactionist Theory is a sociological theory created by George Herbert Mead in the early 1900s.

This theory summarizes that human interaction is based upon shared meaning and understanding. People create their own identities through their social interactions with others. We learn about ourselves, others, and the world through these interactions.

A real-life example of this theory is found in everyday conversation. For example, if two people are having a conversation, they will communicate not just through the words they say but through their body language and facial expressions.

QUESTIONS

1. According to interactionist theory, how have the interactions between your personal characteristics and environmental factors shaped your personal growth, relationships, and experiences?

2. How can understanding interactionist theory help you recognize the complex interplay between individual and contextual factors that shape your life?

3. What strategies can you use to take a more adaptive and balanced approach to the interaction between your personal characteristics and environmental influences?

JUST-WORLD BIAS

This theory was developed by social psychologist Melvin Lerner in the 1980s and asserts that individuals need to believe that the world is fundamentally logical and fair.

This theory explains why people are often so quick to condemn those they consider wrong-doers.

An example of this in everyday life might be when parents deal with their children when they're misbehaving. In these cases, it's easy to think that any negative outcomes their child experiences or takes part in are due to their own bad decisions instead of mitigating factors.

QUESTIONS

1. Can you cite examples in your life where just-world bias, or the belief that people generally get what they deserve, has influenced your thoughts, feelings, or behaviors?

2. How can understanding just-world bias help you recognize and address the potential impact of this bias on your perceptions of yourself and others?

3. What strategies can you use to challenge just-world bias and foster more empathy, compassion, and understanding in your interactions with others?

MASLOW'S HIERARCHY OF NEEDS

Abraham Maslow established the Hierarchy of Needs theory, introduced in his 1943 paper "A Theory of Human Motivation."

The theory suggests that human needs are arranged in a hierarchy, with the most basic physiological needs, such as food, water, and shelter, at the bottom. As these needs are met, higher-level needs such as safety, love and belonging, esteem, and self-actualization become increasingly important.

According to Maslow, individuals must satisfy their basic physiological and safety needs before focusing on achieving higher-level needs. Once these needs are met, individuals strive to fulfill their needs for love and belonging, esteem, and self-actualization, which involve personal growth, creativity, and fulfillment of one's potential.

The five levels of Maslow's Hierarchy of Needs are:

- **Physiological Needs**: These are the most basic needs that a person requires to survive, such as food, water, shelter, and air. Without these needs being met, a person cannot survive

- **Safety Needs**: Once the physiological needs are met, a person's attention turns to safety and security. This includes physical safety, financial security, and protection from harm

- **Love and Belonging Needs**: Once safety needs are met, a person's attention turns to social needs such as love, affection, and a sense of belonging. This includes intimate relationships, friendships, and family
- **Esteem Needs**: Once social needs are met, a person's attention turns to the need for self-esteem and self-respect. This includes recognition, achievement, and status
- **Self-Actualization Needs**: Once all the other needs are met, a person can focus on achieving their full potential and becoming the best version of themselves. This includes creativity, self-expression, and personal growth

An example of this theory in action might be seen in the workplace. If an employee struggles to make ends meet, they may primarily focus on meeting their basic needs for food, shelter, and safety. Once these needs are met through a steady income, they may become more concerned with developing relationships with coworkers and seeking recognition and growth opportunities within the company. Finally, they may strive to achieve self-actualization by pursuing meaningful work aligning with their values and beliefs.

QUESTIONS

1. How have the various levels of Maslow's hierarchy of needs, from physiological to self-actualization, affected

your personal growth and priorities throughout your life?

2. How can understanding Maslow's hierarchy of needs help you identify and address unmet needs that may be impacting your well-being and relationships?

3. What strategies can you use to ensure you address each level of need to promote personal growth, balance, and self-actualization?

OUTGROUP BIAS THEORY

Henri Tajfel and John Turner 1979 first published Outgroup Bias Theory. This theory attempts to explain how individuals view the social and cultural in-groups and out-groups compared to one another. It suggests that humans tend to prefer members of their own in-group and express a bias towards out-groups and the members belonging to them. This bias can be observed through psychological and sociological behaviors, such as the distorted perception of out-group members, avoiding interaction with the out-groups, and exhibiting prejudicial behavior towards them.

One example of outgroup bias can be observed in an educational institute setting, where two distinct and different in-groups can be based on their religious background or social status. For example, students from a lower-income background and those from a higher-income background. Students from higher-income backgrounds may show an outgroup bias towards lower-income students by treating them differently, showing prejudice, and expressing a lack of social or cultural acceptance.

QUESTIONS

1. Can you give examples from your life where outgroup bias, the tendency to view members of other groups

negatively, has affected your thoughts, feelings, or behaviors?

2. How can understanding outgroup bias theory help you recognize and address the potential impact of this bias on your relationships and interactions with others?

3. What strategies can you use to address out-of-group bias and promote greater inclusivity, empathy, and understanding across groups?

PSYCHOLOGICAL SAFETY

Amy Edmondson's concept of Psychological Safety is crucial for understanding team dynamics and effective collaboration. It refers to an environment where individuals feel safe to take risks, voice their opinions, and admit mistakes without fear of embarrassment or retribution. This safety is essential for fostering open communication, innovation, and learning. In personal relationships, Psychological Safety allows individuals to express themselves openly and honestly, leading to deeper understanding and stronger bonds. When people feel psychologically safe, they can share their thoughts and feelings without fear of judgment, leading to more authentic and supportive relationships.

In the workplace, Psychological Safety is critical for team performance, particularly in high-stakes or creative environments. Teams that feel safe are more likely to bring diverse ideas to the table, challenge the status quo, and learn from each other. Leaders play a key role in creating this safe space by encouraging open dialogue, showing vulnerability, and appreciating diverse perspectives.

QUESTIONS:

1. Reflect on your personal relationships: How does the level of Psychological Safety affect your ability to communicate and resolve conflicts?

2. In what ways can you, as a team member or leader, contribute to building a psychologically safe environment at work?

3. Can you identify actions or behaviors that undermine Psychological Safety? How can you address these to foster a more inclusive and open environment?

SELF-DETERMINATION THEORY

It was developed by Edward L. Deci and Richard M. Ryan, psychologists at the University of Rochester.

SDT is based on the belief that people are naturally motivated to learn, grow and reach their full potential.

The theory proposes that people are motivated by three innate psychological needs: autonomy, competence, and relatedness.

Autonomy refers to the need to feel in control of one's own life and to have a sense of self-determination. Competence refers to the need to feel capable and effective in one's actions and to experience growth and learning. Relatedness refers to the need to feel connected to others and to experience a sense of belonging.

According to SDT, when these three needs are met, individuals experience a sense of well-being and intrinsic motivation, which leads to positive outcomes such as greater happiness, creativity, and achievement. However, when these needs are thwarted or unmet, individuals may experience negative outcomes such as anxiety, depression, and feelings of helplessness.

In real life, an example of how SDT fits is when a student is studying for an exam. If the student is extrinsically motivated, they may be preparing to get a good grade. If they are introjectedly motivated, they may be doing so to avoid the guilt of doing poorly. Meanwhile, intrinsically motivated students may do so because they genuinely enjoy the subject.

QUESTIONS

1. According to self-determination theory, how have your innate psychological needs for autonomy, competence, and relatedness influenced your personal growth, motivation, and well-being?

2. How can understanding self-determination theory help you identify and remove obstacles to meeting these psychological needs in your life?

3. What strategies can you implement to promote greater autonomy, competence, and connectedness in your personal and professional life based on the principles of self-determination theory?

SOCIAL EXCHANGE PROCESS THEORY

This theory by Thibaut & Kelley was developed through observational studies and experiments in 1961. One of the earliest studies involved analyzing the exchanges between a landlord and tenants. The researchers found that tenants who received more benefits from the landlord (e.g., repairs and improvements) were more likely to remain in the building and pay rent on time. Additionally, tenants who felt they were being treated unfairly by the landlord were more likely to engage in negative behavior such as vandalism.

This theory suggests that people in relationships exchange different "goods," such as love, respect, money, and attention, which satisfy both parties' needs and wants.

One example of how this theory is applicable in real life is a romantic relationship. In this type of relationship, partners will have expectations of each other such as showing love, support, care, and respect. As a result, each partner is willing to give the other the desired goods in exchange for benefits and long-lasting loyalty. However, if these expectations are unmet or an individual feels they are not receiving enough in return, they may become unsatisfied and decide to end the relationship.

QUESTIONS

1. How have the principles of Social Exchange Process Theory impacted your understanding of interpersonal relationships? Reflect on a particular relationship where the exchange of emotional, social, or material resources has either strengthened or weakened your connection. What does this reveal about your expectations and contributions in relationships?

2. In what ways can understanding Social Exchange Process Theory help you identify and address imbalances in your personal relationships or life choices? Consider situations where you've felt either overburdened or underappreciated. How might this theory guide you in making adjustments for more fulfilling and equitable exchanges?

3. What strategies can you implement in your professional life to foster a more balanced and mutually beneficial exchange of resources, be they emotional support, recognition, or material benefits? Reflect on your current professional relationships: Are there imbalances that need addressing, and how might the principles of Social Exchange Process Theory guide you in creating a healthier work environment?

SOCIAL EXCHANGE THEORY

Social exchange theory by George Homans proposes that social behavior is based on an exchange of rewards and costs between individuals. Homans conducted a study in the 1950s on social exchange among college students. The study showed that students were more likely to form relationships with individuals who provided them with the most rewards, such as friendship or academic assistance. The theory suggests that individuals are constantly weighing the costs and benefits of social interactions and will choose to engage in behaviors that provide the most rewards.

This theory could be witnessed in the workplace. For example, if an employee works diligently but feels inadequately compensated, they may leave the job and seek a work situation with greater rewards. The employee is weighing the costs and rewards of continuing the working relationship and deciding that the costs outweigh the rewards, leading to the decision to leave the job.

QUESTIONS

1. How have the principles of social exchange, such as reciprocity and balance, affected the development and maintenance of your relationships according to social exchange theory in developmental relationships?

2. How can understanding this theory help you identify and address imbalances or areas of dissatisfaction in your developmental relationships, such as mentoring or coaching relationships?

3. What strategies can you implement to promote healthier, more balanced developmental relationships based on the principles of social exchange?

SOCIAL IDENTITY AND SELF-CATEGORIZATION THEORY

John Turner first published the social identity and self-categorization theory in 1979. It seeks to explain how individuals make sense of themselves and their relationships with other people. The idea is that an individual's identity is shaped by how they think about and categorize themselves according to the social groups they identify with. People use these categories to define themselves regarding their similarities and differences with others. Examples of social categories can include age, gender, occupation, race, ethnicity, religious affiliation, and nationality.

The core premise of social identity and self-categorization theory is that an individual's self-concept is heavily influenced by the groups to which they belong. Individuals can establish a sense of belonging and meaningful social connections by offering a positive outlook on their group membership and emphasizing their similarities to others. This theory also highlights how people may distance themselves from other groups, a phenomenon known as "othering."

An example of this occurs when someone moves to a new area. To form a positive identity, the individual might find social groups to join based on areas of similarity, such as interests, hobbies, or shared beliefs. Then, as they engage with their new social circle, they define themselves more accurately, thus establishing a sense of belonging in their new environment.

QUESTIONS

1. How has your identification with certain social groups (like your nationality, profession, or hobby communities) shaped your self-concept and your interactions with others? Reflect on a specific instance where your sense of belonging to a group influenced your behavior or perspective in a social setting.

2. In what ways can recognizing the principles of Social Identity and Self-categorization Theory help you understand your own behavior and attitudes towards different social groups? Consider a scenario where your affiliation with a particular group led to a sense of 'othering' towards those outside the group. How did this affect your perception and actions?

3. What strategies can you implement to utilize the insights from Social Identity and Self-categorization Theory in fostering more inclusive and diverse environments in your professional and social life? Reflect on your workplace or social circles: Are there tendencies to form in-groups and out-groups, and how might this awareness guide you towards more inclusive practices?

SOCIAL IDENTITY PROCESS THEORY

Social identity process theory (SIPT) is a contemporary intergroup theory developed in 1979 by Henri Tajfel and John Turner. It suggests that people strive to maintain and enhance their self-image by enhancing their perception of a group membership.

SIPT explains how group dynamics, intergroup behavior, and perceptions are formed. It proposes that to enhance self-esteem, individuals will identify with social groups that enable them to evaluate themselves positively. A person's perception of their group membership is affected by the group's perceived social identity and its attainability. According to SIPT, various motivational forces determine how individuals form, maintain and enhance their self-perception through social identity, including In-group favoritism, Out-group derogation, Prejudice, and Discrimination.

An example of how SIPT works is an individual belonging to an ethnic minority group who endorses their group by displaying a 'proud' attitude in public. SIPT would support this as it seeks to explain the increased self-confidence they experience by behaving favorably towards their group. This strengthened sense of self-esteem can further enable that individual to build positive relations and engage in successful intergroup experiences.

QUESTIONS

1. How have social identity and self-categorization processes, such as group membership and social comparison, affected your personal growth, relationships, and well-being?

2. How can understanding social identity theory help you recognize the impact of group dynamics and identity on your thoughts, feelings, and behaviors?

3. What strategies can you use to create a healthy balance between your social identity and personal development and to foster positive intergroup relationships?

SOCIAL IMPACT THEORY

Social Impact Theory (also known as the Social Influence Theory, originally developed by Bibb Latané and John Darley, was first published in the 1970s. It explains how people interact with others in a group setting. This theory seeks to explain a person's different influences within a grouping when an opinion or a perspective is shared.

One example of this theory in action can be seen in the workplace. Employees may initially express individual opinions and approach tasks differently. Still, as the team becomes more established and comfortable, a certain set of standards and rules of behavior become common among the group members. As the group norms evolve, the individual opinion of each team member can fall by the wayside, and eventually, it becomes the accepted behavior within the workplace.

QUESTIONS

1. How have the principles of social impact theory, such as the strength, immediacy, and number of sources of influence, affected your thoughts, feelings, and behaviors in different situations?

2. How can understanding social influence theory help you recognize and manage the potential impact of

social influence on your personal development and relationships?

3. What strategies can you use to cope with the influence of social influence and make more autonomous decisions in your personal and professional life?

SOCIAL INFLUENCE THEORY

This theory by Muzafer Sherif, Solomon Asch, and Stanley Milgram explores how the opinions and behaviors of others influence individuals. One famous study conducted by Asch in the 1950s involved a group of participants who were asked to identify the length of a line compared to three other lines. The majority of the group intentionally gave incorrect answers, and the results showed that participants were more likely to conform to group opinion when the group was unanimous in their response. This study demonstrated the power of group pressure and social conformity.

An example of Social Influence Theory is when friends decide to go to a certain restaurant. Everyone knows the popular restaurant, so they all agree to go there. As a result, each person's individual opinion of the restaurant is influenced by the opinions of the rest of the group.

QUESTIONS

1. Can you give examples from your life in which social influence, or the way other people influence your thoughts, feelings, and behaviors, has played an important role?

2. How can understanding social influence theory help you recognize and manage the potential impact of social pressure and conformity on your personal development and relationships?

3. What strategies can you use to combat the negative effects of social influence and promote greater self-awareness and authenticity in your interactions with others?

SOCIAL LEARNING THEORY

Albert Bandura first proposed this theory in 1977. It posited that learning was a cognitive process that took place in a social context and was centered around the observation of behavior, the retention of information, and the subsequent behavior's imitation.

It explains how people learn new things by observing what others do. According to Bandura, humans are both influenced by their environment and have the capacity to make changes and shape their environment. This theory focuses on learning within a social context. It considers how another person's observed behavior can shape an individual's attitudes, motivation, and behavior.

One example of how Social Learning Theory is applicable in real life is through observational learning. This involves watching and imitating another person's behavior, which could be an authority figure or a peer. An example of this is a child seeing their parent clean their room, and they then imitate their behavior and begin to clean their own room. This type of learning could have a powerful effect on developing good behavior, character, and socialization.

QUESTIONS

1. Can you give examples from your life in which social learning or the process of learning by observing and imitating others has influenced your thoughts, feelings, or behaviors?

2. How can understanding social learning theory help you recognize and manage the potential impact of modeling and reinforcement on your personal growth and relationships?

3. What strategies can you use to optimize your social learning experiences and cultivate positive habits and skills based on the principles of social learning theory?

SOCIAL LEARNING THEORY OF CAREER DECISION MAKING

Dr. Marcia Sacks established the Social Learning Theory of Career Decision Making (SLTCDM). This theory posits that individuals are not just passively learning career skills and knowledge but actively integrating information from their social environment.

For example, a young individual who has parents who work in the medical field may be more likely to consider trying a career in health care themselves. This is because the child has been repeatedly exposed to that and its jargon and has learned key skills and information from their parents.

QUESTIONS

1. How have social learning experiences, such as observing and emulating others' career choices, influenced your own career decision-making process?

2. How can understanding social learning theory in career decision making help you identify and manage the potential impact of social influences on your career choices and satisfaction?

3. What strategies can you use to make more informed
    and autonomous decisions based on the principles of
    social learning theory in career choice?

SOCIAL PERCEPTION THEORY

Social Perception Theory was developed by Gordon Allport and Floyd Allport and published in 1967. This theory claims that people form impressions of others in two ways. The first is through direct cues, such as physical appearance and verbal statements. The second way is through inferences based on the other person's behavior. The idea is that people are actively trying to make sense of the behavior of others to feel part of a socially cohesive group.

A job interview setting is one example of how this theory applies in real life. During a job interview, the interviewer is likely to form an impression of the potential employee based on how they present themselves, their words, and their behavior. In this case, the interviewer is gathering cues from the interviewee to form a perception of that person. They may also make assumptions about the person based on their body language, such as feeling uneasy or uncomfortable, to draw further conclusions about the interviewee's character.

QUESTIONS

1. How have your social perception processes, i.e., the way you interpret and understand other people's behavior, influenced your personal development, relationships, and experiences?

2. How can understanding social perception theory help you recognize and address the potential impact of biases and heuristics on your judgments and interactions with others?

3. What strategies can you use to promote more accurate and empathetic social perception in your personal and professional life?

SOCIAL REPRESENTATION THEORY

This theory was first published in the late 1950s by a French sociologist, Serge Moscovici. Social Representation Theory states that any social phenomenon is understood and communicated through sharing a set of beliefs, values, and norms in a collective communication structure.

This theory argues that beliefs, values, and norms within a certain culture are the fundamental components of any social representation. Through this collective communication, people can share common knowledge and understanding of social phenomena. Social Representation Theory further posits that individual members of society actively participate in forming their social representation by individually contributing and constructing meaning.

One example of Social Representation Theory being applicable in real life is the perception of cultural stereotypes. Social Representation Theory states that cultural stereotypes are shared, unconsciously accepted elements of culture and serve as a socially accepted representation of a certain group.

QUESTIONS

1. How have social representations, i.e., shared beliefs and values in your cultural and social context,

influenced your personal development, relationships, and experiences?

2. How can understanding social representation theory help you identify and manage the potential impact of cultural and social factors on your thoughts, feelings, and behaviors?

3. What strategies can you use to challenge and expand your social representations and promote greater under-standing and inclusivity in your personal and profes-sional life?

SOCIOCULTURAL THEORY

The Russian psychologist and socio-cultural theorist Lev Vygotsky developed this theory in the early 20th century.

This theory posits that learning is an inherently social process where knowledge is acquired and developed through social interactions. It suggests that an individual's learning is heavily influenced by whatever culture the person inhabits and is a result of their specific social experiences. Therefore, learning is a combined effort between the learner and those around him or her, such as parents, teachers, peers, etc.

A real-life example of this theory could be seen in a kindergarten classroom. Say the teacher provides a nurturing and supportive environment where young students can develop their cognitive skills by collaborating effectively with their peers. This environment allows students to learn from one another and the teacher, thereby applying the Sociocultural Theory in real-world scenarios.

QUESTIONS

1. How have sociocultural factors, such as cultural, social, and historical contexts, influenced your personal growth, relationships, and experiences?

2. How can understanding sociocultural theory help you recognize and address the potential impact of these factors on your thoughts, feelings, and behaviors?

3. What strategies can you use to deal with and manage the sociocultural factors in your life more effectively and adaptively?

STEREOTYPING

Stereotyping is the theory and practice of ascribing certain traits associated with a particular group of people to an individual. Stereotyping is often based on oversimplified generalizations, leading to social prejudice and discrimination. This term was first coined in 1922 by British journalist Walter Lippmann.

Stereotyping is an example of an unfounded belief, often based on experience, without questioning accuracy or facts.

Real-life examples of stereotyping include gender roles, where it is common to assume that men are more 'masculine' and women are more nurturing. Racial and ethnic stereotypes, like assuming that all Asian people are smart or that only African Americans like rap music.

QUESTIONS

1. Can you cite examples in your life where stereotypes or overly generalized and simplified beliefs about groups of people have influenced your thoughts, feelings, or behaviors?

2. How can understanding the process of stereotyping help you recognize and address the potential impact of stereotypes on your personal growth and relationships?

3. What strategies can you use to challenge and overcome stereotypes to promote greater empathy, understanding, and inclusivity in your personal and professional life?

134

SOCIAL COMPARISON AND DEPRESSION THEORY

Social comparison and depression theory was introduced by Blascovich & Tomaka in 1948. This theory states that when an individual looks to others for comparison to assess their self-worth and how others see them, they could conclude that they fall short compared to these other individuals.

People who are prone to depression may engage in social comparison more often, and may be more likely to compare themselves to others who they perceive to be better off than themselves. This can lead to feelings of inadequacy, low self-esteem, and hopelessness.

Furthermore, social comparison can contribute to a negative feedback loop. For example, a person who feels down may compare themselves to someone who appears to be happier or more successful. This comparison can make them feel even worse, which leads to further negative comparisons and a further decline in mood.

However, it is worth noting that social comparison is not always negative. Positive social comparison, in which a person compares themselves to someone who they perceive to be worse off, can lead to feelings of gratitude, contentment, and increased self-esteem.

One example of how this theory applies in real life is when an individual compares their financial status to their neighbor. If their neighbor is more wealthy than them, this individual may end up concluding that they are not successful. These feelings of being inadequate can result in depressive symptoms.

QUESTIONS

1. Are there instances in your life where social comparison or the tendency to evaluate yourself in comparison to others has led to depression or feelings of inadequacy?

2. How can understanding social comparison theory and depression help you recognize and manage the potential impact of social comparison on your mental health and well-being?

3. What strategies can you use to minimize the negative effects of social comparison and promote a self-compassionate and growth mindset?

SOCIAL COMPARISON AND GROUP POLARIZATION THEORY

The Social Comparison and Group Polarization Theory was proposed in 2001 by Muzafer Sherif. He suggests that people in a group tend to compare themselves, increasing their commitment to their pre-existing views. This theory further proposes that the individuals will look at the group to determine how strongly they should feel about an issue. For example, if everyone else in the group is generally in agreement, then the individual will double down on their commitment to their point of view.

One example of how the Social Comparison and Group Polarization Theory is applicable in real life is the behavior of football fans in a stadium. Studies have illustrated that crowd mentality has a profound effect on football fans, causing them to conform to the behaviors of the larger fan base in the stadium.

QUESTIONS

1. Reflect on a situation where your opinions or beliefs were influenced by the dominant views of a group you were part of. How did the process of social comparison within this group affect your stance on a particular issue? Did you find your views becoming more extreme or polarized due to the group's influence?

2. In what ways can recognizing the dynamics of Social Comparison and Group Polarization help you understand your decision-making process in social settings? Consider a time when you conformed to a group's opinion or behavior. How might awareness of this theory influence your future interactions and decisions in similar situations?

3. What strategies can you implement to mitigate the effects of group polarization in your professional environment? Think about instances in your workplace where groupthink or polarization may have influenced decisions or behaviors. How can you encourage more balanced and independent thinking within teams to avoid the pitfalls of extreme group consensus?

SOCIAL COMPARISON AND MOTIVATION

This theory was developed by social psychologists Santos & Mountcastle in 1954. It suggests that individuals are motivated by comparing themselves to others, both consciously and unconsciously. This comparison is used to evaluate attitudes, opinions, and behaviors and to form judgments and opinions of oneself.

Real-life examples of social comparison and motivation could include a student being motivated to earn better grades because they compare themselves to their peers or an employee striving for a promotion because of the perceived success of their co-workers. As humans continually strive for relevance and acceptance, social comparison theory motivates them to reach the desired level of success.

QUESTIONS

1. How has social comparison, the tendency to evaluate yourself in comparison to others, affected your motivation and goal setting in various areas of your life?

2. How can understanding the relationship between social comparison and motivation help you identify and address the potential impact of social comparison on your personal growth and goal achievement?

3. What strategies can you use to promote a more intrinsic and self-focused approach to motivation and goal setting and minimize the influence of social comparison?

SOCIAL COMPARISON AND WELL-BEING THEORY

This theory by Festinger proposes that social comparison can have both positive and negative effects on psychological well-being. For example, individuals may experience social comparison upward (comparing themselves to those who are better off) and feel motivated to improve themselves. However, individuals may also experience downward social comparison (comparing themselves to those who are worse off) and feel a boost in self-esteem. The theory suggests that individuals may benefit from using social comparison in a strategic and mindful way.

For example, a student may compare their academic performance to that of their peers, in which case someone with a higher score is likely to have positive feelings and a stronger sense of self-efficacy. In comparison, someone with a lesser score is likelier to feel inferior, discouraged, and dissatisfied. Social comparison can then profoundly affect how an individual views and experiences their world.

QUESTIONS

1. Reflect on a recent situation where you engaged in upward or downward social comparison. How did this comparison affect your feelings of self-worth, motivation, or satisfaction? Did it inspire you to improve, or did it lead to feelings of inadequacy?

2. How can being aware of the effects of social comparison help you in managing your emotional responses and aspirations? Think about instances where comparing yourself to others has either positively or negatively impacted your drive for personal growth. How might a more strategic and mindful approach to social comparison benefit you?

3. What strategies can you adopt to use social comparison constructively in your professional and social life? Consider how comparing yourself to colleagues or peers can be a source of motivation rather than a cause for dissatisfaction. How can you balance the natural tendency to compare with a healthy perspective on personal and professional development?

SOCIAL COMPARISON THEORY

American social psychologist Leon Festinger proposed this theory in 1954. Its main premise is that individuals evaluate their own opinions and abilities by comparing themselves to others. As people compare themselves to others, they gain a sense of understanding about what is acceptable or desirable for them. Furthermore, this evaluation of themselves allows them to adapt their behaviors and beliefs to fit into the established social framework.

For example, an individual may choose to increase the amount of physical activity to fit in with the rest of society's health and fitness standards. This is done by comparing one's lifestyle to the general population's. If an individual finds that their diet and exercise habits are not up to par with the rest of the population, they may strive to change their behaviors and beliefs to fit in socially.

QUESTIONS

1. How has social comparison, the process of assessing yourself in comparison to others, affected your personal growth, relationships, and experiences?

2. How can understanding social comparison theory help you recognize and address the potential impact of social comparison on your thoughts, feelings, and behaviors?

3. What strategies can you use to minimize the negative effects of social comparison and promote a self-compassionate and growth mindset?

THE SOCIAL IDENTITY THEORY OF INTERGROUP BEHAVIOR

Henri Tajfel and John Turner first proposed the Social Identity Theory (SIT) of intergroup behavior in 1979. It has become one of the main theories of intergroup relations. SIT is based on the idea that individuals derive their social identities from their membership in a social group and that intergroup behavior is shaped by the individual's attempts to enhance their standing among the groups with whom they identify.

SIT explains that people identify with groups to feel accepted and appreciated in order to gain a sense of self-worth. When this group identity is threatened or challenged, intergroup behavior can become too hostile to maintain its position as the "in" group. For example, students in a school setting may display intergroup behavior when a rival school is seen as a threat. They may express their in-group identity by engaging in activities such as taunting, name-calling, or even resorting to physical violence to protect their identity.

This theory can be applied in the real world to better understand how individuals and groups interact. For example, it can explain why two different cultural groups might conflict with each other, even in the same country. The underlying mechanisms of intergroup behavior suggest that people rely on identifying with their group to maintain a strong social identity, producing hostile behavior towards other competing groups.

QUESTIONS

1. Reflect on a time when your social identity, derived from a group you belong to, significantly influenced your behavior or attitude towards another group. How did your affiliation with this group shape your perceptions and actions towards members of an 'out-group'?

2. How can an understanding of the Social Identity Theory help you navigate and comprehend conflicts or biases in your personal or social life? Think about instances where group identity may have played a role in creating divisions or misunderstandings between different communities or social circles.

3. What strategies can you implement to mitigate the negative aspects of intergroup behavior in your professional environment or community based on the principles of SIT? Consider how awareness of group identities and the desire for positive self-concept can influence interactions and how fostering a more inclusive and understanding environment can counteract tendencies towards hostility or bias.

THEORY OF PLANNED BEHAVIOR

The Theory of Planned Behavior, developed by Icek Ajzen, posits that behavior is determined by the intention to perform the behavior. It explains human actions by three key factors:

1. Attitude toward the behavior: An individual's personal evaluation (positive or negative) of the behavior. For example, someone may believe a new career path leads to growth, creating a positive attitude towards changing careers.

2. Subjective norms: The perceived social pressure to perform or avoid the behavior. If significant others encourage a career change, the individual might feel more inclined to pursue it.

3. Perceived behavioral control: This is about how easy or difficult one perceives the behavior to be, based on resources, skills, and opportunities. Believing one can successfully transition to a new career increases the likelihood of intending to do so.

This theory can be applied to understanding how we form intentions and how these intentions translate into action. For instance, an individual's decision to pursue a new career path might be influenced by personal attitudes, societal expectations, and the perceived ease or difficulty of making the career change.

QUESTIONS:

1. Think of a behavior or goal you are working towards. How do your attitudes, the perceived social norms, and your perceived control over the behavior affect your intention to pursue this goal?

2. How can the Theory of Planned Behavior inform your approach to setting and achieving professional goals?

3. What can you do to positively influence your attitudes, perceived norms, and control to foster personal growth and achieve your desired outcomes?

DECISION MAKING AND LEADERSHIP THEORIES

BASE RATE NEGLECT THEORY

Base Rate Neglect as theory first appeared in a 1988 study by Kahneman and Tversky, two aforementioned and renowned cognitive psychologists. The theory states that people tend to pay more attention to specific information or data, incorrectly assuming that it is more relevant, instead of paying attention to other context-based information. This phenomenon is known as base rate neglect, in which individuals ignore more pertinent information, such as base rates when making decisions.

One example of this is when people use heuristics and make decisions without considering essential factors. For instance, when reading about a job opening for an engineer, a person may focus on the data saying that 85% of the current engineers employed by the company have a degree from a specific college and assume that a degree from this specific college is necessary to get the job, when in fact, the base rate indicates that only 4% of the engineers with a degree from this college are working at the company.

QUESTIONS

1. Can you give examples in your life where you have neglected basic information or the general frequency of an event in favor of more vivid or specific information?

2. How can understanding base rate neglect theory help you recognize and manage the potential impact of this cognitive bias on your decision making and judgment?

3. What strategies can you use to improve your decision making and judgment by considering base rate information and mitigating the impact of base rate neglect?

DUAL-PROCESS THEORY

This theory, that was primarily popularized by Daniel Kahneman, distinguishes between two types of thinking: System 1 and System 2. System 1 is fast, automatic, and often unconscious, enabling quick judgments and intuitive decisions. It operates with little effort and doesn't require deliberate control. In contrast, System 2 is slow, effortful, deliberative, and logical. It's used in situations that require careful thought, complex computations, or when learning new activities.

In Kahneman's influential book "Thinking, Fast and Slow" published in 2011, he extensively discussed this theory, although the roots of the concept can be traced back to earlier psychological research. System 1 encompasses instinctive reactions and snap judgments, often based on learned heuristics or biases, while System 2 involves analytical and critical thinking, engaging in more rational and structured decision-making processes. This dual-process model has been instrumental in understanding various aspects of human behavior, including decision-making, problem-solving, and reasoning.

QUESTIONS:

1. Can you identify a recent decision where you relied primarily on instinct (System 1) versus a logical analysis (System 2)? How did each approach impact the decision?

2. In your career, how can you balance quick, instinctive decisions with more thoughtful, analytical approaches?

3. What steps can you take to ensure that you're using the appropriate system of thinking for different situations in your life?

ESCALATION OF COMMITMENT

The phrase "escalation of commitment" was first used by Barry M. Staw in 1976 and further developed by Nobel Laureate Herbert A. Simon. The theory states that when individuals become invested in a decision, they are often unable to walk away, even when the decision is no longer beneficial.

Essentially, the concept of escalation of commitment explains why organizations and individuals may continue to pursue a course of action even when it is not yielding positive results.

For example, imagine you're a business investor who has invested a lot of money into a particular venture. You start to see that the venture is not yielding the expected return on investment. Still, instead of pulling out your investments and creating a different strategy, you willingly continue to contribute more time and money in the hope that you'll disprove the initial evidence and make the venture successful.

QUESTIONS

1. Can you cite examples in your life where you have experienced escalation of commitment, i.e., the tendency to continue to invest in a decision or course of action based on the sunk costs already incurred?

2. How can understanding engagement escalation help you identify and address the potential impact of this phenomenon on your decision making and resource allocation?

3. What strategies can you use to minimize the impact of engagement escalation and make more rational, evidence-based decisions in your personal and professional life?

EXPECTANCY THEORY

Expectancy Theory is a motivation theory developed by psychologist Victor Vroom in 1964. The theory suggests that an individual's behavior is a consequence of their expectations about the outcomes of that behavior.

Suppose a student aims to get accepted into a good college. In that case, they may be more motivated to stay up late studying, despite the difficulty, because they believe that if they work hard, they will be accepted into their college of choice. Similarly, an employee might put in the extra effort on a project due to the perceived reward, whether a promotion, a raise, or simply an acknowledgment of their hard work.

QUESTIONS

1. How do your expectations, i.e., the beliefs you hold about the likelihood of achieving certain outcomes, influence your motivation and goal setting in various aspects of your life?

2. How can understanding expectancy theory help you identify and address the potential impact of expectations on your personal growth and goal achievement?

3. What strategies can you use to foster realistic and growth-oriented expectations while maintaining high levels of motivation and commitment to your goals?

FRAMING EFFECT

Amos Tversky and Daniel Kahneman first proposed the concept of the framing effect. The framing effect influences decisions based on how a situation is presented to an individual. Specifically, the theory suggests that a decision's outcome is heavily influenced by how the information is presented or 'framed' to the individual.

For example, if an individual is presented with two options: Option A, receiving a sure reward of $100, or Option B, having a 50% chance of receiving $200, most people will prefer Option A as it is deemed to be the safer option, with a guaranteed reward. However, if the second option is framed differently and instead presented as Option B, with a 50% chance of losing $200, then most people will prefer Option A. Although both choices represent the same underlying risks, the framing effect influences an individual's decision by showing that what an individual values highly depends on how the consequential information is presented.

Real-life examples of the framing effect can be found in areas such as marketing. For example, a supermarket might offer a product with a 'buy one get one free' promotion, encouraging customers to purchase. The product is presented to the consumer as a desirable offer that is framed in a positive light. Alternatively, the same product could be sold by offering '50% off' on the second purchase. In this instance, the framing effect is highlighted by how simply changing how the sale is presented non-substantively encourages customers to purchase.

QUESTIONS

1. Can you give examples from your life where the framing effect, the way information is presented, has influenced your decisions and judgments?

2. How can understanding the framing effect help you recognize and address the potential impact of this cognitive bias on your decisions and judgments?

3. What strategies can you use to minimize the influence of the framing effect and make more objective, evidence-based decisions in your personal and professional life?

GOAL SETTING THEORY

Goal setting theory is a psychological theory established by Edwin A. Locke, which emphasizes the importance of setting specific, challenging, attainable goals to reach higher performance. This theory is centered on the belief that when individuals are provided with specific, challenging goals, they become more motivated to achieve them.

For example, an individual may set a goal to lose weight by a certain date, but the goal may not be achieved without a clear plan of how to reach it. In addition, with periodic feedback and rewards, the individual will be more likely to stay motivated to reach their goal.

QUESTIONS

1. Can you give examples from your life where goal setting has positively or negatively affected your motivation, performance, or personal development?

2. How can understanding goal setting theory help you identify and address the potential impact of effective goal setting on your personal and professional development?

3. What strategies can you use to set SMART (Specific, Measurable, Achievable, Relevant, Time-bound) goals that align with your values, priorities, and aspirations and foster a sense of purpose and direction in your life?

GROWTH MINDSET

Developed by Carol Dweck, the concept of a Growth Mindset is central to understanding how individuals perceive their abilities and intelligence. Unlike a Fixed Mindset, where abilities are viewed as innate and immutable, a Growth Mindset embraces the idea that skills and intelligence can be developed through effort, learning, and persistence.

In the context of personal relationships, a Growth Mindset can lead to healthier and more resilient connections. For example, when facing communication challenges in a relationship, individuals with a Growth Mindset are more likely to view these challenges as opportunities to develop and enhance their communication skills. They are more open to feedback, less defensive, and more willing to make changes for the betterment of the relationship.

In a professional setting, a Growth Mindset can be transformative. It encourages a culture of continuous learning, where mistakes are viewed as opportunities for growth rather than failures. Employees are more likely to seek out challenges, persist through difficulties, and embrace lifelong learning. This mindset fosters innovation and adaptability, which are crucial in today's rapidly changing work environments.

QUESTIONS:

1. Think about a time when you faced failure or criticism in a personal relationship. How might a Growth Mindset have changed your response and the eventual outcome?

2. How can embracing a Growth Mindset in your workplace lead to more effective problem-solving and innovation?

3. What are some daily practices or affirmations you can adopt to cultivate and reinforce a Growth Mindset?

HYPERBOLIC DISCOUNTING

Hyperbolic discounting is a theory of decision-making developed by Richard Thaler in 1981. It states that people prefer an immediate reward over a larger one in the future. In other words, people have a lower threshold for accepting a reward if it is available immediately rather than after a delay.

An example of this theory in real life would be someone skipping a workout or study session today for the immediate gratification of sitting around and watching TV instead.

QUESTIONS

1. Have you experienced hyperbolic discounting in your life, i.e., the tendency to prefer smaller, immediate rewards to larger, later-arriving rewards?

2. How can understanding hyperbolic discounting help you recognize and manage the potential impact of this cognitive bias on your decision making and achievement of long-term goals?

3. What strategies can you use to overcome the influence of hyperbolic discounting and make more balanced, long-term decisions in your personal and professional life?

JOB CHARACTERISTICS MODEL

The Job Characteristics Model, also called JCM, was established and published by Edgar H. Schein in 1985. This theory is also known as the Motivator-Hygiene Theory or The Three-Factor Theory. The Job Characteristics Model presents a very prospective approach to motivating employees in the workplace. The summary of this theory, put simply, is that core job dimensions tend to have a profound effect on an employee's motivation, satisfaction, and performance.

An example of a real-life application of the Job Characteristics Model would be a call center representative. By giving the call center representative more autonomy, the scope of their job can become more meaningful to them as they will have more freedom in helping customers.

QUESTIONS

1. What impact do the five key job characteristics (skill diversity, task identity, task importance, autonomy, and feedback) have on your job satisfaction, motivation, and performance?

2. How can understanding the job characteristics model help you identify and address the potential impact

of job design on your professional development and well-being?

3. What strategies can you use to improve key workplace characteristics in your current role or when seeking new career opportunities, promoting greater job satisfaction and personal growth?

JOB DEMANDS-RESOURCES THEORY

University of Utrecht professor and researcher Christina Maslach established the Job Demands-Resources Theory (also known as JD-R Theory) in 2001.

The theory posits that when the workload on a job becomes too high or an employee has too few resources to effectively complete their tasks, the job can start to become overwhelming. This can lead to lower work motivation and job satisfaction. On the other hand, when the resources provided are sufficient, job satisfaction and performance can increase.

A real-life example of this theory can be seen in the hospitality industry. The demands of a job in the hospitality industry can be very high due to long working hours, long shifts, and customer demands. However, these demands can be balanced if the employee has sufficient resources. This could include access to a breakroom or helpful support from managers and colleagues.

QUESTIONS

1. How do work demands, i.e., the physical, psychological, social, or organizational aspects of your job that require sustained effort, and work resources, i.e., the aspects that help you achieve your work goals and reduce work demands, affect your well-being and work performance?

2. How can understanding the theory of work demand-sand resources help you identify and manage the potential impact of work demands and resources on your career development and well-being?

3. What strategies can you use to optimize the balance of work demands and resources in your work environment to promote greater job satisfaction and personal growth?

NEGLECT OF INFORMATION

Neglect of information refers to the tendency to overlook or ignore relevant information presented to us. This theory suggests that when individuals face too much information, they can often overlook important details associated with the decision-making process. Behavioral psychologist Richard Nisbett first introduced the neglect of information in 1975.

Someone may be attracted to the discounted price of a product and overlook important details, such as the product's quality or functionality. When faced with a barrage of information, individuals often focus on the most salient and obvious information rather than all relevant details.

QUESTIONS

1. Can you cite examples in your life where you consciously or unconsciously neglected important information when making decisions or judgments?

2. How can understanding information neglect help you recognize and address the potential impact of this cognitive bias on your decisions and judgments?

3. What strategies can you use to ensure that you consider all relevant information when making decisions and judgments, minimizing the impact of information neglect?

NEGLECT OF PROBABILITY

The founder of the Neglect of Probability theory is cognitive psychologist Daniel Kahneman.

The Neglect of Probability theory, also called the "neglect heuristic" or the "probability neglect hypothesis," suggests that people can overlook the importance of probability when making decisions. Kahneman theorized that individuals often focus too heavily on the easier-to-identify cues associated with an event or situation rather than considering the probability of the event's occurrence.

For example, an individual might assume that because something has never happened to them before, it will never happen in the future. This assumption, however, overlooks that although the event has not happened, the probability of it occurring is still present.

QUESTIONS

1. Can you give examples from your life where you have failed to consider the probability of different outcomes when making decisions or judgments?

2. How can understanding probability neglect help you recognize and address the potential impact of this cognitive bias on your decisions and judgments?

3. What strategies can you use to better incorporate probability information when making decisions and judgments and minimize the impact of probability neglect?

NEGLECT OF REGRESSION

The founder of this theory was Francis Galton 1889.

This concept suggests that when faced with something threatening or uncomfortable, people tend to revert to simpler behaviors and responses used in earlier stages of development to regain feelings of safety and security.

An example of this theory can be seen when a parent is confronted with an emotionally overwhelmed child. Instead of calmly reasoning with them and teaching them to manage their emotions, the parent may give in to their demands and act in a way that is more reminiscent of a child's way of thinking.

QUESTIONS

1. Can you cite examples in your life where you have not considered the phenomenon of regression to the mean, or the tendency for extreme outcomes to be followed by outcomes closer to the mean, when making decisions or forming judgments?

2. How can understanding regression neglect help you recognize and address the potential impact of this cognitive bias on your decisions and judgments?

3. What strategies can you use to better consider the concept of regression to the mean in decision making and judgment formation and minimize the impact of regression neglect?

OPTIMISM BIAS THEORY

Optimism bias refers to the tendency of individuals to overestimate the likelihood of positive events and underestimate the likelihood of negative events. A study by Shelley E. Taylor and Jonathan D. Brown found that individuals often hold optimistic beliefs about their health, such as underestimating their risk of illness or injury. This bias can lead to positive outcomes such as increased motivation and resilience but can also result in poor decision-making if it leads individuals to underestimate risks.

An example of Optimism Bias Theory in action is that of a person believing they will not suffer any major consequences if they operate a car after a few drinks. However, in reality, the person might be unaware of the potentially serious consequences they will face.

QUESTIONS

1. Reflect on a decision you made where optimism bias may have played a role. Did this bias lead you to underestimate the risks or overestimate the positive outcomes? How did this decision impact your life, and what did you learn from this experience about balancing optimism with realism?

2. How can an awareness of optimism bias help you in assessing your own attitudes towards challenges and setbacks in your life? Consider situations where maintaining a positive outlook benefited you, and contrast these with instances where an overly optimistic view might have led to poor outcomes. How might you use this understanding to strike a balance between optimism and practicality?

3. What strategies can you implement to counteract the potential negative effects of optimism bias in your professional decisions and everyday activities? Think about scenarios where a realistic assessment of risks and challenges is crucial. How can you cultivate a mindset that is both optimistic and grounded in realistic expectations?

OVERCONFIDENCE BIAS

The tendency to be more confident in one's abilities and decisions than is warranted by the available evidence was first studied by Gary Klein in 1995. In one of his studies, firefighters were asked to estimate how long it would take them to complete various firefighting tasks. The results showed that they consistently overestimated their abilities, leading to longer completion times than they had anticipated.

An example of how this theory applies in real life is that an individual may think their football team is a clear favorite to win an upcoming competition. This individual might make a judgment, such as betting all their money on their team winning the competition, based on an inaccurate estimation of their ability. The team would then lose, resulting in a financial loss for the individual.

QUESTIONS

1. Can you give examples from your life in which overestimating yourself or the tendency to overestimate your own abilities, knowledge, or skills has influenced your decision making or judgment?

2. How can understanding self-overestimation help you recognize and manage the potential impact of this cognitive bias on your decisions and evaluations?

3. What strategies can you use to more accurately calibrate your self-confidence and ensure that it matches your actual skills and knowledge, both in your personal and professional life?

SELF-EFFICACY THEORY

Self-Efficacy Theory is a social cognitive theory created by American psychologist Albert Bandura in the 1970s. This theory believes everyone can self-regulate their behaviors and motivations to achieve their goals.

The theory states that individuals acquire a sense of self-efficacy by observing the behaviors of others, performing repetitive tasks and being given feedback, and mastering challenges by showing their capabilities.

Self-efficacy beliefs are shaped by four primary sources of information: mastery experiences (i.e., successfully performing a task or behavior), vicarious experiences (i.e., observing others successfully perform a task or behavior), social persuasion (i.e., receiving encouragement or feedback from others), and physiological and emotional states (i.e., physical and emotional reactions to a task or behavior).

Research has shown that higher levels of self-efficacy are associated with a range of positive outcomes, including higher levels of motivation, greater persistence in the face of challenges, better task performance, and improved emotional well-being. On the other hand, lower levels of self-efficacy are associated with lower levels of motivation, reduced persistence, poorer task performance, and increased risk of developing mental health problems such as depression and anxiety.

For example, in educational settings, those with higher levels of self-efficacy are likely to engage more with their studies and peers and have a better sense of agency in their learning.

QUESTIONS

1. How do you rate your current self-efficacy, i.e., your belief that you are able to successfully perform tasks and achieve goals, in various areas of your life (e.g., personal growth, relationships, career)?

2. How can understanding self-efficacy theory help you identify and address the potential impact of self-efficacy on your motivation, resilience, and overall well-being?

3. What strategies can you implement to improve your self-efficacy and / or cultivating a sense of empowerment in your personal and professional life?

STRENGTHS-BASED APPROACH

The Strengths-Based Approach, pioneered by psychologist Donald O. Clifton in the late 20th century, focuses on identifying and leveraging an individual's core strengths rather than fixing their weaknesses. This approach, widely popularized in the realms of personal development and organizational leadership, stems from the idea that people grow and excel more when they build on their natural talents.

Under this approach, the key is to first identify one's innate strengths, often through assessments like the CliftonStrengths (formerly StrengthsFinder) tool. Once these strengths are recognized, individuals are encouraged to cultivate and apply them in various aspects of their lives. For example, if a person's primary strength is empathy, they might be guided to use this trait to enhance their relationships or to excel in roles that require understanding and connecting with others.

In a professional setting, this approach can transform how teams function. Instead of trying to remedy each team member's weaknesses, leaders using a strengths-based approach align tasks and roles with the natural strengths of team members. This alignment not only boosts productivity and engagement but also enhances overall job satisfaction.

The Strengths-Based Approach has been influential in shifting the focus from what is wrong to what is strong, fostering a more positive and productive environment in both personal and professional contexts. It's a valuable tool for self-improvement, team building, and leadership development.

QUESTIONS:

1. How can embracing a Strengths-Based Approach in your personal relationships improve your interactions and deepen your connections, especially when you focus on recognizing and appreciating the inherent strengths of those around you?

2. In your career, how can identifying and leveraging your core strengths, as per the Strengths-Based Approach, enhance your performance and job satisfaction, particularly in roles that align with your natural talents?

3. What steps can you take to adopt a Strengths-Based Approach in your personal development journey, focusing on cultivating and applying your strengths to overcome challenges and achieve your goals?

SUNK COST FALLACY

The Sunk Cost Fallacy is a theory established by American economist and Nobel Laureate Richard H. Thaler in 1986. This theory states that individuals' decisions are typically affected by what they have already invested in a venture, regardless of the actual value of the current decision concerning their expected outcomes. In other words, individuals often continue to invest in an endeavor or option, even if it is no longer the most sensible or optimal choice, due to their prior investment.

For example, someone may continue investing in a failing project or stock, despite other, more desirable options simply because they have already invested substantial money and/or time. In this case, they allow the previous investment to drive future decision-making at the expense of more unfettered and rational decision-making.

This theory implies that individuals should consider the prospects of each investment objectively without attaching special value to prior efforts that have already been sunk into a project.

QUESTIONS

1. Can you cite examples in your life where you have fallen prey to the sunk cost fallacy, i.e., the tendency to continue to invest in a decision or course of action based

on the resources already invested rather than evaluating current and future value?

2. How can understanding the sunk cost fallacy help you recognize and manage the potential impact of this phenomenon on your decision making and resource allocation?

3. What strategies can you use to minimize the impact of the Sunk Cost Fallacy and make more rational, evidence-based decisions in your personal and professional life?

TERROR MANAGEMENT THEORY

Terror Management Theory was established by Sheldon Solomon, Jeff Greenberg, and Tom Pyszczynski in the late 20th century.

The theory suggests that humans have an innate fear of death, which creates anxiety managed through cultural beliefs and worldviews. According to Terror Management Theory, individuals use their cultural beliefs, values, and worldviews as a buffer against the anxiety caused by the awareness of their mortality. An example of this theory in action might be seen in a person experiencing anxiety about their mortality. They may cope with this anxiety by reaffirming their cultural beliefs and values, such as religious or political beliefs, to find meaning and purpose in life. Alternatively, individuals may engage in defensive or aggressive behaviors toward those who hold different beliefs to protect their worldview and buffering against their fear of death.

QUESTIONS

1. How do thoughts about your own mortality or the inevitability of death influence your behavior, decision making, and relationships with others?

2. How can understanding terror management theory help you recognize and manage the potential impact of mortality expectations on your personal growth, values, and priorities?

3. What strategies can you use to better manage existential concerns and live a meaningful, fulfilling life in the face of mortality?

THE CURSE OF KNOWLEDGE

The founder of this theory is Dr. Elizabeth Newton, a graduate student at Stanford University in 1990. Her findings summarize that people who possess knowledge about a subject are often unable to see the subject from the perspective of the uninitiated. Consequently, people with knowledge find it difficult to accurately convey what they know to the uninitiated without extra effort.

An example of this theory in real life would be an experienced computer programmer trying to explain a complex concept to someone without prior knowledge of computer programming. The experienced individual might assume that because they are familiar and comfortable with the subject, everyone else is as well. This can lead to difficulty understanding and communicating the concept, resulting in frustration.

QUESTIONS

1. Can you give examples from your life where the curse of knowledge, or the difficulty of understanding or communicating information from the perspective of someone with less knowledge, has affected your interactions with others?

2. How can understanding the curse of knowledge help you recognize and manage the potential impact of this cognitive bias on your communication and relationships?

3. What strategies can you use to overcome the curse of knowledge and effectively share your knowledge or experience with others without neglecting their perspective?

THE DUNNING-KRUGER EFFECT

David Dunning and Justin Kruger 1999 first described the Dunning-Kruger effect. Participants were asked to rate their skills and abilities in various areas of their study. The results showed that participants who scored the lowest in a particular area tended to overestimate their abilities, while those who scored the highest tended to underestimate their abilities.

The Dunning-Kruger Effect is a cognitive bias in which people with low ability or knowledge in a particular domain overestimate their own competence and performance, while those with high ability or knowledge underestimate their own competence and performance.

This can lead to overconfidence and a lack of awareness of one's own limitations, which can have negative consequences in various areas of life, such as decision-making, problem-solving, and learning.

The Dunning-Kruger Effect is often cited in discussions related to education, politics, and social media, as it can help explain why some people may confidently express opinions or make claims that are not supported by evidence or expertise.

A real-life example of the Dunning-Kruger effect can be seen in someone who has just started learning to play an instrument. They may have a limited understanding of the complexity of the skill, leading them to overestimate their ability to play.

This could result in them performing poorly in front of others or making mistakes they did not anticipate. However, as they become more experienced and learn more about the intricacies of playing the instrument, they can begin to realize the extent of their limitations and start to accurately assess their skill level.

QUESTIONS

1. Are there instances in your life where the Dunning-Kruger effect, the tendency of people with low skills or knowledge in a particular area to overestimate their competence, has influenced your decisions or judgments?

2. How can understanding the Dunning-Kruger effect help you recognize and manage the potential impact of this cognitive bias on your personal growth and development?

3. What strategies can you use to more accurately calibrate your self-assessment and foster a growth mindset in which you continually seek to learn and improve in different areas of your life?

THE ENDOWMENT EFFECT

This theory originates from an experiment created by Richard Thaler and Daniel Kahneman in the late 1980s. This theory posits that when people acquire something, they tend to work diligently to protect it and view it as having greater value than the same item to others in a non-ownership position.

A real-life example of this theory can be seen when people go to an auction. When bidders already own an item placed on the auction block, they may be willing to bid more to keep the item as they decide they already have a connection. However, other bidders, who don't have that connection, consider the item as less valuable.

QUESTIONS

1. Can you give examples in your life where the endowment effect, the tendency to value things more highly simply because you own them, has influenced your decisions or judgments?

2. How can understanding the endowment effect help you recognize and manage the potential impact of this cognitive bias on your decisions, evaluations, and resource allocation?

3. What strategies can you use to minimize the influence of the endowment effect and make more rational, evidence-based decisions in your personal and professional life?

THE FALSE CONSENSUS EFFECT

The False Consensus Effect is a cognitive bias observed in social psychology, introduced in 1977 by Lee Ross, a social psychologist at Stanford University. It is the tendency to overestimate how people around us share our beliefs, opinions, and behaviors. This bias is grounded in our inherent desire to feel secure and accepted among our peers and therefore creates an assumption that others think and act just as we do.

For example, if the consensus in a certain group of people appears to agree on certain beliefs, the members of this group tend to falsely assume that outsiders hold the same beliefs. This phenomenon is also seen when someone is unhappy with their current situation, as they tend to overestimate the number of others who are unhappy and/or in the same situation.

QUESTIONS

1. Can you give examples from your life in which the false consensus effect, i.e., the tendency to overestimate the extent to which others share your beliefs, attitudes, or preferences, has influenced your decisions or judgments?

2. How can understanding the false consensus effect help you recognize and manage the potential impact of this

cognitive bias on your interactions and relationships with others?

3. What strategies can you use to more accurately assess the beliefs, attitudes, and preferences of others and promote a more open and empathetic approach to communication and relationship building?

THE FALSE MEMORY EFFECT

Elizabeth Loftus first studied the false memory effect in the 1970s. In her studies, participants were shown pictures and then asked to recall the pictures they had seen. Later, they were shown new pictures and some original pictures and were asked to identify which pictures they had seen before. In some cases, participants identified pictures they had not seen similar to the ones they had seen earlier. This demonstrated that the information provided after an event can alter or distort a person's memory of the event.

Eyewitness testimony is often used in court cases, but research has shown that it is not always accurate. The false memory effect can explain why a witness may recall seeing something that did not occur or why their memory of an event can change over time.

QUESTIONS

1. Can you give examples from your life in which you have had false memories, that is, memories of events that did not happen at all or happened differently than you remember?

2. How can understanding the effect of false memory help you recognize and manage the potential impact of

this cognitive distortion on your interpretations of past experiences and relationships with others?

3. What strategies can you use to improve the accuracy of your memory and better distinguish between correct memories and possible false memories?

THE FALSE UNIQUENESS EFFECT

The false uniqueness effect is a psychological phenomenon first identified by David Dunning and Justin Kruger in 1999. It is the idea that people tend to overestimate the uniqueness of their traits and abilities while simultaneously underestimating the number of people with similar traits or abilities. Essentially, it involves the overestimation of one's specialness or sense of importance relative to others.

For example, a person may feel that the ability to play an instrument is rare, despite countless other people playing the same instrument. Similarly, students may feel that their grade in a particular class sets them apart, despite many peers achieving the same grade.

One explanation for the false uniqueness effect is the tendency for individuals to remember that they possess certain skills while disregarding the fact that many other people can also possess those skills. This can lead to an inflated idea of one's importance and ability in a particular area. In real life, this translates to people believing that their accomplishments are more extraordinary than those of others.

QUESTIONS

1. Can you give examples in your life in which the effect of false uniqueness, i.e., the tendency to underestimate the extent to which others share your positive qualities or abilities, has affected your perception of yourself or your judgment of others?

2. How can understanding the effect of false uniqueness help you recognize and address the potential impact of this cognitive bias on your personal growth, self-esteem, and relationships with others?

3. What strategies can you use to more accurately assess your own positive attributes and abilities in comparison to others to promote a more balanced and realistic self-perception?

THE NEGLECT OF SECONDARY EFFECTS

The Neglect of Secondary Effects, a theory proposed by psychologist Richard E. Nisbett, is based on the idea that people tend to focus mainly on the primary causes of any change or event and neglect to consider or remember the secondary causes.

It suggests that humans are attracted to causal explanations with a single component, such as environmental versus genetic factors, rather than considering multiple causes delivered over time.

An example of this in real life can be a baseball game. Fans and commentators tend to attribute the score to the player's performance instead of recognizing that the stadium's environment, field condition, and coaching style can all contribute to the game's outcome.

QUESTIONS

1. Can you cite examples in your life where you have failed to consider secondary effects, that is, the indirect and often unintended consequences of a decision or action?

2. How can understanding the neglect of secondary effects help you recognize and manage the potential impact of this cognitive bias on your decisions and evaluations?

3. What strategies can you use to better anticipate and evaluate the potential secondary impacts of your decisions and actions, allowing for more comprehensive and informed decision making?

THE OBSERVER-EXPECTANCY EFFECT

This effect was first proposed in 1959 by psychologist Robert Rosenthal. It states that when people have a set expectation of a person or situation, their behavior and perception of the results are shaped by that expectation.

If a physician believes a patient may have a certain medical condition, they may look for signs and symptoms supporting that belief. As a result, they could fail to find other serious conditions the patient suffers from.

If a researcher conducting an experiment expects a certain result, they may unintentionally bias their observations or data collection to support that expectation. Similarly, if a teacher believes that certain students are academically gifted, they may unknowingly provide those students with more opportunities and encouragement, leading to better performance.

The Observer-Expectancy Effect can have significant implications for scientific research, education, and interpersonal relationships. To mitigate its effects, researchers and educators should strive to remain objective and impartial, and be aware of their own biases and preconceptions. It is also important to ensure that research methods are rigorous and transparent, so that potential sources of bias can be identified and controlled for.

QUESTIONS

1. Can you give examples from your life in which the observer-expectancy effect, i.e., the influence of an observer's expectations on the outcome of an event or interaction, has affected your behavior or the behavior of others?

2. How can understanding the observer-expectancy effect help you recognize and manage the potential impact of this phenomenon on your expectations, perceptions, and interactions with others?

3. What strategies can you use to minimize the influence of the observer-expectancy effect and promote a more objective and unbiased approach to evaluating situations and interacting with others?

TRANSFORMATIONAL LEADERSHIP THEORY

Transformational Leadership Theory was introduced by James MacGregor Burns in 1978 and further developed by Bernard Bass. It suggests that effective leaders can transform and motivate their followers through charisma, individualized consideration, and intelligence. The theory is based on four key components: Idealized Influence, Inspirational Motivation, Intellectual Stimulation, and Individualized Consideration.

This theory posits that effective leaders should be able to transform and motivate followers through charisma, individualized consideration, and intelligence.

One real-life example of this theory is Steve Jobs, the founder of Apple. He was known for his ability to inspire and motivate his team to create innovative products. He used a combination of Idealized Influence, Inspirational Motivation, Intellectual Stimulation, and Individualized Consideration to lead his team to success.

QUESTIONS

1. Can you cite examples in your life where you have experienced or demonstrated transformational leadership characterized by inspiring, empowering, and motivating others to reach their full potential?

2. How can understanding transformational leadership theory help you recognize and address the potential impact of effective leadership on your personal growth, relationships, and professional success?

3. What strategies can you use to develop and embody transformational leadership skills to foster a positive and supportive environment for yourself and those around you?

THEORY U

Theory U, developed by Otto Scharmer in the early 21st century, is a framework for understanding change and leading transformative processes in individuals, organizations, and social systems. At the heart of Theory U is the concept that the quality of the results we create in any kind of social system is a function of the quality of awareness, attention, or consciousness that the participants in the system operate from.

This theory suggests that by moving down the "U" shape, individuals and groups can shift from reacting based on past patterns to responding creatively from a deeper, more conscious level. The process involves seven stages: Downloading (sticking to habitual judgments), Seeing (suspension of judgments and opening up), Sensing (empathy and seeing from the whole), Presencing (connecting to the deepest source of self and will), Crystallizing (intention for what wants to emerge), Prototyping (exploring the future by doing), and Performing (implementing the new in ecosystems).

For instance, a business leader using Theory U might begin by acknowledging their own preconceived notions and biases. Through a process of deep listening and empathy, they would strive to understand the perspectives of their team and the broader environment. This approach could lead to more innovative solutions that are deeply connected to the core mission and values of the organization.

Theory U is particularly relevant for leading change in complex and challenging times. It encourages leaders and change-makers to be introspective and to connect deeply with their environment, leading to actions that are more aligned with the emerging future.

QUESTIONS:

1. How can applying the stages of Theory U enhance your personal relationships, particularly by moving from habitual reactions to a deeper understanding and connection with your partner or family members?

2. In what ways can the principles of Theory U transform your approach to leadership and innovation within your career, especially by encouraging a shift from operating on autopilot to engaging in creative and conscious decision-making?

3. What practices inspired by Theory U can you integrate into your personal development journey to cultivate a more conscious and intentional approach to life's challenges and opportunities?

MENTIONABLE AND IMPORTANT THEORIES

The theory was established by a German biologist named Ernst Haeckel in the late 1800s, and it is based on a belief that all life forms can be traced back to a single common ancestor.

This theory is important in the scientific world as it outlines a framework for understanding the relationships between all living organisms. A real-life example of this theory is in the process of speciation, or when a new species is formed through the genetic isolation of a larger population. This process is seen as a result of the genetic diversity the common ancestor provides, but it is not necessarily the only explanation. The Biological Theory identifies how life forms evolve and adapt to their environment.

QUESTIONS

1. How do you think your biological factors such as genetics, brain chemistry and physical health have influenced your personality, behaviour and mental well-being?

2. How can understanding the biological theory of psychology help you identify and address the potential impact of biological factors on your personal growth, relationships and overall well-being?

3. What strategies can you use to optimise your physical health and well-being, potentially positively impacting your mental health?

COGNITIVE THEORY

Jean Piaget established the Cognitive Theory in the 1930s.

This theory summarizes that cognitive theory is focused on understanding how people learn, think, solve problems and use knowledge in their daily lives. The main components of cognitive theory are the processes of understanding and actively transforming information through language and other cognitive tools. In addition, it explains the mental processes that determine how we perceive, remember, and construct reasoning and problem-solving examples.

A real-life example of this theory is using verbal language to solve problems. For example, suppose you were to try and determine the answer to a mathematical problem. In that case, cognitive theory highlights that transforming words into solution-oriented information is the key to the answer.

QUESTIONS

1. How have your cognitive processes, such as perception, memory and problem solving, influenced your personal development, relationships and professional success?

2. How can understanding cognitive theory help you identify and address the potential impact of cognitive

processes on your mental wellbeing and overall quality of life?

3. What strategies can you implement to improve your cognitive abilities, fostering a more efficient and adaptive approach to processing information and navigating challenges in life?

EXISTENTIAL PSYCHOLOGY

Existential Psychology, significantly shaped by thinkers like Rollo May and Irvin Yalom, delves into the depths of human existence. Developed during the mid-20th century, this branch of psychology focuses on understanding the human condition through concepts such as the search for meaning, the confrontation with existential isolation, and the inevitability of death.

At the core of Existential Psychology is the belief that individuals are continually in the process of making choices that shape their existence. It emphasizes the capacity for self-awareness and the freedom to make choices, despite inherent life constraints. For instance, when facing a career crossroads, an individual practicing the principles of Existential Psychology might ponder the meaning and purpose of each path, rather than merely considering external factors like income or prestige.

This psychological perspective also highlights the importance of facing anxieties and existential dilemmas head-on. It encourages individuals to embrace their freedom and responsibility to make meaning in their lives. By doing so, one can live more authentically, aligning actions with personal values and beliefs. Existential Psychology offers valuable insights into living a fulfilling life, particularly in navigating life's inevitable challenges and existential questions.

QUESTIONS:

1. How can applying the principles of Existential Psychology in your personal relationships deepen your connections, considering the emphasis on authentic living and the honest confrontation of existential dilemmas can enhance mutual understanding and respect?

2. Considering Existential Psychology's focus on the freedom to make choices and the search for meaning, how can this perspective influence your career decisions, especially when evaluating paths that align with your core values and beliefs rather than external rewards?

3. What practices inspired by Existential Psychology can you adopt to more actively confront and embrace life's existential challenges, thereby promoting personal growth and a more meaningful existence, especially in light of the understanding that facing anxieties and existential questions head-on can lead to a more authentic life?

FLOW THEORY

Flow Theory, introduced by Mihaly Csikszentmihalyi in the 1970s, describes a psychological state in which an individual is fully immersed and engaged in an activity, leading to a sense of enjoyment and fulfillment. This state, often referred to as being 'in the zone,' is characterized by a seamless flow of action and awareness, where a person loses the sense of self-consciousness, time becomes distorted, and the activity becomes rewarding in itself.

A typical example of this is an artist who becomes so absorbed in painting that they lose track of time and are completely engrossed in the creative process. This experience of Flow is not just limited to creative activities; it can be experienced in various domains, including sports, writing, or even everyday tasks that present a balance of challenge and skill. Csikszentmihalyi's research emphasized that achieving this state of Flow is a key component of happiness, productivity, and personal fulfillment.

QUESTIONS:

1. Think of a time when you were completely absorbed in an activity. How did it affect your relationship with the task and your sense of fulfillment?

2. How can the concept of flow enhance your productivity and satisfaction in your career?

3. What strategies can you implement to more frequently achieve a state of flow in your personal or professional life?

NEUROPSYCHOLOGY THEORY

Neuropsychology Theory was established by the French philosopher Rene Descartes in the 16th century.

This theory explains how mental processes are related to the anatomy and functioning of the brain. The brain is the source of all thinking, feeling, and behavior, and by analyzing its activity, we can better understand human cognition, emotion, and behavior.

A real-life example of this theory is that people with damage to the frontal lobe of their brain are often unable to make decisions, while people with damage to the temporal lobe may have impaired memory. By studying the various functions of the brain, we can learn more about how the different structures of the brain lead to specific behaviors.

QUESTIONS

1. What impact do you think the structure and function of your brain has on your personality, behavior, and mental well-being?

2. How can understanding neuropsychological theory help you identify and address the potential impact of brain-related factors on your personal growth, relationships, and overall well-being?

3. What strategies can you implement to optimize your cognitive functioning, potentially influencing your psychological health in a positive way?

SELIGMAN'S POSITIVE PSYCHOLOGY

Martin Seligman established Positive Psychology in the late 1990s.

The theory suggests that psychology should also promote well-being and happiness instead of treating mental illness. Positive Psychology focuses on building positive emotions, developing strengths and virtues, and promoting meaning and purpose in life.

An example of this theory in action might be seen in a person struggling with depression. With the help of Positive Psychology interventions, a therapist can work with the individual to identify and cultivate positive emotions and character strengths, such as gratitude and perseverance. The therapist can also help the individual develop a sense of purpose or meaning in life, such as finding a fulfilling job or engaging in activities that bring them joy. By focusing on these positive aspects of life, the individual can increase their overall sense of well-being and reduce symptoms of depression.

QUESTIONS

1. Can you give examples in your life where cultivating positive emotions, engaging in meaningful activities,

or cultivating positive relationships have contributed to your well-being and personal development?

2. How can understanding Seligman's principles of Positive Psychology help you to recognise and address the potential impact of positive psychological factors on your overall quality of life?

3. What strategies can you use to integrate the principles of positive psychology into your daily life to promote a greater sense of well-being, resilience and fulfillment?

SKINNER'S OPERANT CONDITIONING

B.F. Skinner established Operant Conditioning in the mid-20th century.

The theory suggests that behavior is shaped by its consequences, specifically through reinforcement and punishment. According to Skinner, behavior followed by a desirable consequence (reinforcement) is more likely to be repeated. In contrast, behavior followed by an undesirable consequence (punishment) is less likely to be repeated.

An example of this theory in action might be seen in a parent who wants to encourage their child to do well in school. The parent might offer positive reinforcement, such as a reward or praise, for good grades or completing homework on time. On the other hand, they might also use punishment for poor grades or failing to complete homework, such as taking away privileges. With these methods, the parent can shape the child's behavior and encourage them to succeed academically.

QUESTIONS

1. Can you give examples from your life in which operant conditioning, the process of learning through consequences such as reinforcement or punishment, has influenced your behavior or the behavior of others?

2. How can understanding Skinner's operant conditioning theory help you recognize and address the potential impact of this learning process on your personal growth, relationships, and overall well-being?

3. What strategies can you employ to effectively use the principles of operant conditioning to promote desirable behaviors and prevent undesirable behaviors in your personal and professional life?

THEORY OF MIND

David Premack and Gail Woodruff developed the Theory of Mind in the late 20th century.

The theory suggests that humans can attribute mental states, such as beliefs, desires, and intentions, to themselves and others. According to the Theory of Mind, individuals use their understanding of mental states to predict and explain behavior and to communicate effectively with others.

The theory of mind is an important cognitive skill that helps us to navigate social interactions and relationships. It allows us to understand and predict the behavior of others, communicate effectively, and form social bonds. It is also closely linked to empathy, as the ability to understand and appreciate the mental states of others is a key aspect of empathetic behavior.

The development of the theory of mind is a gradual process that starts in early childhood and continues into adolescence and adulthood. Infants and toddlers start to develop an understanding of basic emotions and desires, and gradually become more adept at interpreting and predicting the thoughts and intentions of others.

An example of this theory in action might be seen in a child playing with a toy and pretending that it is alive. The child uses their mind to attribute mental states, such as beliefs and desires, to the toy and act accordingly. Their ability to understand and apply this concept is an important aspect of their cognitive development and social interactions.

QUESTIONS

1. How would you rate your ability to understand and empathize with the thoughts, feelings, and perspectives of others, also known as "Theory of Mind"?

2. How can understanding the concept of Theory of Mind help you recognize and address the potential impact of empathic understanding on your relationships and social interactions?

3. What strategies can you use to improve your Theory of Mind and foster a greater sense of empathy, understanding, and connection with others?

GENERAL QUESTIONS FOR GROWTH

These are some extra coaching, mind expanding, and goal setting questions that you could ask yourself about the aforementioned or other theories that you might find interesting:

1. How does this theory affect or play out in your life?

2. How can you use the insights of this theory to benefit your personal growth, relationships, or career?

3. What could be a reachable goal for you when using the insights of this theory?

4. What resources do you have helping you to master life with the help of this theory?

5. Now, what is the first step of reaching that goal?

CONCLUSION

This guidebook has offered you comprehensive insights to help you transform your life and achieve personal growth. Throughout the book, you have delved into the world of psychology and gained knowledge that will enable you to take control of your life.

By exploring more than 100 scientific theories, including cognitive-behavioral therapy, emotional intelligence, and positive psychology, you have gained a deeper understanding of yourself and your behaviors. This guidebook has provided you with an in-depth examination of these theories and practical examples to help you overcome obstacles and improve your life.

As you have progressed through each chapter, you have been empowered to take a proactive approach to your personal growth. By embracing the concepts outlined in each chapter and putting them into practice, you can make significant strides toward becoming the best version of yourself.

Overall, "Master Your Life - Psychologically: Grow in Life through 100+ Scientific Theories" is an invaluable guidebook for anyone looking to improve their life, understand themselves, and achieve personal growth. Its comprehensive exploration of scientific theories, combined with real-life examples, makes it an essential resource for anyone seeking to transform their lives and achieve their goals. Keep this book by your side on your journey to mastering your life psychologically.

REFERENCES

Brown, J. D. (1986). Evaluations of self and others: Self-enhancement biases in social judgments. Social Cognition, 4, 353-376.

Campbell-J. D. (1986). Similarity and uniqueness: The effects of attribute type, relevance, and individual differences in self-esteem and depression. Journal of Personality and Social Psychology, 50, 281- 294.

Carlson- C. R., & Masters4 J. C. (1986). Inoculation by emotion: Effects of positive emotional states on children's reactions to social comparison. Developmental Psychology, 22, 760-765.

Cash, T. E, Cash- D. W., & Butters, J. W. (1983), "Mirror, mirror, on the wall... ?": Contrast effects and self-evaluations of physical attractiveness. Personality and Social Psychology Bulletin, 9, 351 - 358.

Cialdini i R. B., & Richardson, K. D. (1980), Two indirect tactics of impression management: Basking and blasting. Journal of Personality and Social Psychology, 39, 406-4 15.

Conway, M., & Ross, M. (1984), Getting what you want by revising what you had. Journal of Personality and Social Psychology, 47, 738- 748.

Crocker, J., & Gallo, L. (1985, August). The self-enhancing effect of downward comparison: Paper presented at the meeting of the American Psychological Association, Los Angeles, CA. Crocker, J., Thompson- L. L., McGraw, K. M., & Ingerman- C. (1987). Downward comparison prejudice and evaluations of others: Effects of self-esteem and threat. Journal of Personality and Social Psychology, 52, 907-916.

Crosby, E (1976). A model of egoistical relative deprivation. Psychological Review, 83, 85-113.

Dakin, S., & Arrowood, A. J. (1981). The social comparison of ability. Human Relations, 34, 89-109.

Dadey, J. M., & Goethals, G. R. (1980). People's analyses of the causes of ability-linked performances. In L. Berkowitz (Ed.), Advances in experimental social psychology (pp. 1-37). New York: Academic Press.

Davis- J. A. (i 966). The campus as a frog pond: An application of the theory of relative deprivation to career decisions of college men. American Journal of Sociology, 72, 17-3 l.

Deutsch, M., & Krauss, R. M. (1965). Theories in socialpsychology New York: Basic Books.

Diener, E. (1984). Subjective well-being. Psychological Bulletin, 95, 542-575.

Feldman, N. S., & Ruble, D. N. (1977). Awareness of social comparison interest and motivations: A developmental study. Journal of Educational Psychology, 69, 579-585.

Feldman- N. S., & Ruble, D. N. (1981). Social comparison strategies: Dimensions offered, and options taken. Personality and Social Psychology Bulletin, 7, I 1-16.

Festinger, L. (1954). A theory of social comparison processes. Human Relations, 7, 117-140.

Fisher, J., Nadl- A., & Whitcher-Alagna, S. (1982). Recipient reactions to aid. Psychological Bulletin, 91, 27-54.

France-Kaatrude, A., & Smith, W. E 0985). Social comparison, task motivation, and the development of self-evaluative standards in children. Developmental Psychology, 21, 1080-1089.

Frey, K. S., & Ruble, D. N. (1985). What children say when the teacher is not around: Conflicting goals in social comparison and performance assessment in the classroom. Journal of Personality and Social Psychology, 48, 550-562.

Friend, R. M., & Gilbert, J. (1973). Threat and fear of negative evaluation as determinants of locus of social comparison, Journal of Personality, 41, 328-340

www.ingramcontent.com/pod-product-compliance
Lightning Source LLC
LaVergne TN
LVHW010320200726
843507LV00010B/1296